SEPHARDI

COOKING THE HISTORY

Cherry
Orchard
Books

SEPHARDI

COOKING THE HISTORY

Recipes of the Jews of Spain and the Diaspora, from the 13th Century to Today

Hélène Jawhara Piñer

Preface by David Gitlitz

Boston
2021

Library of Congress Cataloging-in-Publication Data

Names: Piñer, Hélène Jawhara, author.
Title: Sephardi : cooking the history, recipes of the Jews of Spain and the diaspora, from the 13th century onwards / Hélène Jawhara Piñer.
Description: Boston : Cherry Orchard Books, 2021.
Identifiers: LCCN 2020045212 (print) | LCCN 2020045213 (ebook) | ISBN 9781644695319 (hardback) | ISBN 9781644695326 (adobe pdf) | ISBN 9781644695333 (epub)
Subjects: LCSH: Sephardic cooking. | Jews--Food--History. | LCGFT: Cookbooks.
Classification: LCC TX724.2.S47 P56 2021 (print) | LCC TX724.2.S47 (ebook) | DDC 641.5/676--dc23

LC record available at https://lccn.loc.gov/2020045212
LC ebook record available at https://lccn.loc.gov/2020045213

Third printing, 2021. Printed in China.

Book design by PHi Business Solutions.
Cover design by Ivan Grave.
Cover photo by Hélène Jawhara Piñer.
Interior photos by Hélène Jawhara Piñer.

Publisher by Cherry Orchard Books, imprint of Academic Studies Press.
1577 Beacon St.
Brookline, MA 02446
press@academicstudiespress.com
www.academicstudiespress.com

A mi abuela,
Ana Guillen Palma

In memory of my friend, my mentor,
David Gitlitz

CONTENTS

FOREWORD

Like many cookbooks, the one that you have in your hands is a miscellany. Unlike most of them, you will find that this one comes with a heart, a spine, a soul. Its spine is the resilience of a thousand years of Sephardi cooks, living in minority enclaves surrounded by powerful, attractive, and frequently unfriendly majority cultures; cooks who retained the essence of their Jewish culinary heritage and transmitted it from mother to daughter, and sometimes even from parents of both genders to their diverse children. Its heart beats to the rhythms of the Jewish week and liturgical year, Shabbat, Sukkot, Pesach, Yom Kippur, the fasts and feasts, the tables around which Jewish families gathered from season to season and from century to century. Its soul is nurtured in a faith that despite the hatred and fear, the Inquisitions and the pogroms, the silent discriminations and the seductive attractions of assimilation, the kitchens of Sephardi descendants in Spain, in Portugal, and in all the lands of the great Sephardi diaspora are, and will forever be, cooking Jewish.

Hélène Jawhara Piñer is perhaps uniquely prepared to confect this cookbook. She is an accomplished chef and an experienced communicator. Her doctorate, from the French University of Tours, acknowledges her work in two intimately intertwined fields, medieval history and the history of food. Her skills as both a chef and teacher have been frequently showcased at festivals and on television.

Most of us are familiar with the broad outlines of the history of the Jews of Spain and Portugal. How their origin dates back to second century Roman expulsion of the Jews from Jerusalem and Palestine. How these displaced Jews often struggled during their early centuries in the Iberian Peninsula under Romans and Visigoths, and how they thrived during the 800-year rule by Muslim kingdoms. How the tiny Christian enclaves in the peninsular north resisted the Muslims and gradually pushed south and grew into the large kingdoms of Castile and Aragon, and their smaller neighbors Navarre and Portugal. How the Jews who had now come to be living under Christian rule were increasingly persecuted. How when in the late 1400s Castile and Aragon united under Ferdinand and Isabel, the self-styled Catholic Monarchs, Jews were offered the choice of conversion or exile. And how the religious behavior of those who chose to convert and remain as Christians was rigorously policed by the Inquisition.

We tend not to be familiar, however, with the rich and complex culinary traditions of the Iberian Peninsula, its mixture of Celtic, Iberian, Roman-Mediterranean, Germanic, and North African styles and flavors and aromas. Iberian Jews steeped themselves in these traditions and then did what Jews have always done. Using the ingredients at hand at the particular time and place where they happened to be living, they adapted these local cuisines to the Jewish dietary restrictions, and created from them their everyday meals, their Sabbath stews, and their special flavors and treats for the cycle of Jewish holidays. Few scholars are as immersed in the history and the particulars of these adaptations as is Hélène Piñer.

The beauty of this book is the way that Hélène explains the culinary world of medieval Iberian Jews and, with examples and anecdotes, brings those long-ago cooks to life. She almost always draws her material from contemporary medieval sources, gleaned from data found in documents written in more languages than many of us speak, always with the goal of creating tasty representative recipes that can be prepared in modern kitchens by cooks at any level of culinary skill.

That's the first half of the book. In the second, Hélène's curiosity journeys to the Jews of the Sephardic diaspora, the countries where the Spanish and Portuguese exiles settled. There, just as in their ancestral homes in Iberia, they incorporated the products and techniques of those new lands into their repertoire of Sabbath and holiday creations. And lastly, as if to exemplify for us this centuries-old pattern of relocation, adaptation, and creation, Hélène treats us to a few recipes—very traditional and yet brand new—that she has created in her own kitchen.

So… read, and cook, and enjoy! Wrap your nose around the aromas of far-off spice markets and bubbling Sabbath stews. Treat your tongues to the flavors of Sephardic history.

Bon appetit! Buen provecho! !בתאבון

David Gitlitz

INTRODUCTION

This cookbook is unique. It is not based on family recipes but on the history of the Jewish people from Spain, and by extension the Sephardim, from the thirteenth century to the present day. It is a cookbook derived from historical sources—be they culinary, judicial, literary, or medical—from the East and the West. Its recipes were prepared over five years as part of my doctoral research in history, which traces and uncovers the existence of dishes prepared for and by Sephardic Jews. This is also a cookbook that reveals social issues of the time: the vast majority of these dishes were prepared in societies rife with anti-Semitism, where food served as a tool to denounce the liturgical practices of the Jews.

Origin

Sephardi: in order to understand the subject of this cookbook, we need to remember what this term means. *Sefarad* is the Hebrew word for "Spain." The name goes back to the book of Obadiah (עובדיה) verse 20, where the terms "Tsarfat" and "Sefarad" appear:

וגלת החל–הזה לבני ישראל אשר–כנענים עד צרפת, וגלת ירושלים אשר בספרד ירשו ...

Although those terms in context must refer to places in Mesopotamia, in medieval Europe the names *Tsarfat* and *Sefarad* were assigned by Jews respectively and retroactively to France and Spain so as to claim that Jews were present in the West *before* Jesus was crucified, and therefore could bear no responsibility for the act.

Sephardim is the name originally given to the Jews from Spain and Portugal after 1492, and was later applied to all Jews of the Iberian diaspora. *Conversos* referred to anyone who converted, as well as their descendants, regardless of whether they continued to self-identify as Jewish or Christian. The word was used to indicate Jewish ancestry. Initially, at least in theory, it was value-neutral. *Crypto-Jews*, or *Judaizers* (as the Inquisition called them), were newly converted Christians (i.e. *conversos*) who still evidenced Jewish beliefs or practices.

Jews are documented in Iberia from the second century until the fifteenth under Roman, Visigothic, Muslim, and Christian rule. Their living conditions in Christian Spain deteriorated from the eleventh century up until March 31, 1492, when the Alhambra Decree ordered the Jews to either convert or accept expulsion. This act was part of a plan by the Catholic monarchs, Isabella I of Castile and Ferdinand II of Aragon, to unify Spain principally through religion. The Inquisition—aimed at identifying converts who continued to practice their former religion in secret—had been created a few years earlier (1478).

The exiles left Spain initially for Portugal, southern France, Italy, and Morocco, and later for Ottoman Turkey (which included Greece) and other eastern Mediterranean countries. Some also crossed the Atlantic illegally, as Jews were banned from travelling to the territories of the New World. Indeed, one of the main tenets of the Inquisition was to stop Jews from spreading their religion in this "new" part of the world, since the Catholic kings feared this would taint their efforts to convert indigenous peoples to Christianity. However, we know that Sephardi people did cross the Atlantic to Mexico, Brazil, Argentina, the Dominican Republic, and other countries. *Conversos* from the Americas were also called *marranos*, a pejorative term sometimes used to label Sephardic crypto-Jews. *Marranos* are characterized by a mix of Jewish and Catholic practices. Nonetheless, these different factions of Jews are all considered to be Sephardim.

Sources

For more than five years, I have been analyzing the recipes described in the three cookbooks of the Iberian Peninsula: two written in Arabic in the thirteenth century, the *Kitāb al-ṭabīẖ* and the *Fuḍālat al-ẖiwān,* and one written in Catalan in the fourteenth century, the *Sent Soví*, for a total of over a thousand recipes. Throughout the Middle Ages until the nineteenth century, only eight recipes have been found that are specifically identified as "Jewish" in their name. All the information available on Jewish cooking and practices of the time is found in other kinds of sources. The ways we can identify a certain dish as Sephardic lies in how the dish was cooked, the feast for which it was consumed, the way it was prepared, the ingredients it contained, the source of the meat, the type of wine consumed, and so on.

In my research, I carried out a careful reading and meticulous analysis of these recipes and coupled it with the study of other sources: literary (the *Libro de Buen amor*, the *Cancionero de Baena*, the *Copla a Pedro González*, and the *Cancionero general*), scholarly (dictionaries, Humach), medical (the *Regimen of Health* by Maimonides), judicial (Inquisition trials)—all of which reinforce a historical connection with the Jews. This research and cross-breeding of historical sources allowed me to establish links between the dishes and Sephardic culinary techniques. The analysis and comparison of historical sources mentioning these dishes attest to the transmission of these dishes and practices in the Iberian Peninsula as well as around the diaspora today.

Naturally, the way these recipes were compiled and presented in these various sources is very different to what we expect from recipes today. For example, there is rarely any mention of quantities of the various ingredients. It was through a careful comparison of disparate material, coupled with background research on agricultural and medicinal practices, that I was able to piece together how these dishes were made. The aim of this book is to offer as close a reconstruction as possible of what the dishes looked and tasted like, in the tradition of the fascinating and inspiring book *A Drizzle of Honey* by David Gitlitz and Linda Kay Davidson.

I chose not to include foods that did not exist in the territory in question at the time, such as tomato, pepper, potato, or chili, which were not present in the Iberian Peninsula before the sixteenth century and were only regularly consumed a century later; only corn is mentioned, as part of a recipe found in the records of an Inquisition trial in Mexico.

Jewish Holidays

Food and Jewish holidays are interwoven. In Jewish culture, talking about food means talking about religion, and talking about Jewishness means talking about licit and illicit foods. The dietary laws of Kashrut enshrined in the Torah impose a framework for the practice of Judaism. This is also the common thread in the transmission and permanence of culinary uses in the different Jewish communities: all Jewish holidays require specific preparations to be made, including culinary ones, and often involve fasting. This book intends to show how these special culinary traditions and requirements both revealed the Jews' identity to the Inquisition, and allowed it to survive through the centuries.

Shabbat

The place occupied by the Shabbat and the culinary practices of this day of rest, celebrated on the seventh day of each week, is so important that I thought it needed a special explanation. Shabbat begins Friday night before sundown and ends at nightfall on Saturday. During this period, no work—including cooking—is allowed, according to the Torah, and it requires special arrangements that the Inquisition clearly noticed: bringing olive oil to the synagogue, eating cold dishes for lunch on Saturday, cooking in separated pots (e.g., with pork and lard for the non-Jewish servants and without for the Jewish lords), dressing up on Friday night, eating sealed, stuffed dishes that would not reveal their content, and so on. These Shabbat practices were respected by Jews everywhere, and sadly resulted in trials and condemnation on the other side of the Atlantic as well.

Maimonides

Moshe Ben Maimon (1135–1204) is the most famous of the Jewish scholars of Medieval Spain. Known by the acronym RaMBaM or Maimonides, this philosopher, doctor, theologian, and rabbi was born in the city of Cordoba, in Andalusia (southern Spain), at the beginning of the twelfth century. He fled his hometown because of the persecutions of the Berber Almohad dynasty. Exiled in Morocco in 1160, he took refuge in Akko (1165) and Jerusalem. Finally, he moved to Egypt (1166) and ended his days in the city of Fostat. Maimonides wrote on a vast range of topics, all imbued with the Judaism he practiced, such as *Mishneh Torah*, the *Guide for the Perplexed*, and the *Regimen of Health*. It is particularly this latter work that highlights Maimonides' interest in food, medicine, and diet, and it is for this reason, coupled with his living in Spain at the time the *Kitāb al-ṭabīẖ* was written, that he is so important for my cookbook, as he makes recommendations about the diet that everyone should follow to stay healthy.

Inquisition trials

You might wonder how there can be a relation between the Inquisition and the cookbook you hold in your hands. As we mentioned, in 1478, the Spanish monarchs established the court of the Inquisition, which was tasked with investigating and unmasking the *conversos*, or crypto-Jews, who continued to practice Judaism in secret. In particular, the Inquisition targeted celebrations of Jewish religious festivals, as well as adherence to the dietary laws of the Kashrut, to identify and denounce *converso* Jews. The censors collected information on illegal traditions: those who continued to light Shabbat candles on Friday evenings, bring oil to the synagogue, dress in clean clothes on Friday nights, pray in Hebrew, refrain from working on Saturdays, and attending Mass on Sundays were accused of breaking the law.

But another trigger was their culinary practices, which were easily observable and were thought to indicate a latent or a purposeful adherence to the beliefs of their former religion. The Inquisitors were mainly looking at four categories of culinary data: foods that followed Kosher rules like avoiding pork and shellfish; special foods like matza for Jewish holidays; any food prepared on Friday and warmed over to eat on the Shabbat; and any food that was served in conjunction with a Jewish observance, like a birth, wedding, funeral, or concluding a Jewish fast day. The courts then recorded all the facts, noting in writing the food and culinary practices of the Jews: food names, techniques, preparation—everything the Jews ate and the ways in which they ate were recorded during the trials. This is why reading and analyzing the trial records of the Inquisition was a major source for this study. The Spanish records used for this book are those kept at the Archivo Histórico Nacional in Madrid. They mainly concern the northern cities of the territory, such as Ávila, Ciudad Real, Almazán, and Soria, and they are published in the multiple volumes of the *Fontes Iudaeorum Regni Castellae*. As for sources on the Inquisition in Mexico, I used the Archivo General de la Nación of Mexico. Finally, Heitor Furtado de Mendoza's books *Denunciações de Pernambuco (1593–1595)* and *Primeira visitação do Santo Oficio ás partes do Brasil: Denunciações da Bahia (1591–1593)* offered me essential information concerning the Inquisition in Brazil.

My creations

Jewish cuisines are all about adaptation, evolution, and transmission, which is why I decided to also include some of my own original recipes. They are a few samples of dishes made in accordance with the laws of Kashrut and the Jewish holiday traditions, the fruit of my own creativity as a Sephardic chef. Almost all my family members on my mother's side are bakers, pastry chefs, cooks, butchers, or caterers. I inherited my passion for making French pastries from them. On my father's side, my grandmother was and still is an important source of my culinary inspiration, for she is a master at simple and delicious cuisine with a perfect combination of flavors. My ideas also come from meeting other lovers of history and food, particularly during my conference trips: Tel Aviv, São Paulo, Philadelphia, Madrid, Casablanca, and New York are only some of the many cities I traveled to with a wonderfully rich food heritage that fuels my creativity in adapting history to modern flavors. And of course, historical sources are a great part of my inspiration, particularly for holidays such as Shabbat, Yom Kippur, Rosh HaShana, and Shavuot that include some of my favorite foods—eggplant, spinach, olive oil, cheese, bread, coriander, cinnamon, garlic, and honey.

To eat is to remember

This book is the result of five years of doctoral research during which I analyzed more than two thousand different pieces of evidence from different sources relating to Jewish history. For each food category, I include a brief introduction and some reflections on the evolution of the recipes and customs in the Sephardic diasporas. In doing so, I explain the importance of the Jewish holidays and the significance of religion in food and culinary practices. Each recipe is presented, discussed, and illustrated to lend cachet to *Sefarad.*

For me, a dish tastes differently when you know where it really comes from. Its history makes each bite more intense, more delicious.

Sephardi: Cooking the History aims to be the reference cookbook for a sample of recipes of the Jews of Spain and the diaspora from the thirteenth century onwards. It presents the Sephardim of the world as the best representatives and witnesses of a cuisine that continues to live and thrive today.

AMALIO LE HA PUESTO ESTA
CASA A LA GIRALDA
PARA HACERLA SUYA
لقد شاد أماليو هذه الدار
قربانا لمئذنة الجيرالدا
لكي تغدو داره
אמליו בנה את הבית
לכבוד הג'ירלדה
כדי שתהיה שלו

BREAD AND SNACKS

"One of these [beneficial generalizations] is that [among] the good foods that ought to be adopted by everyone who desires the continuation of his health, [is] wheaten bread properly prepared [...]. What I mean by properly prepared bread is that it should be made from fully ripened wheat, dried of its superfluous moisture, in which spoilage from age has not begun. The bread should be made of coarse flour; that is to say, the husk should not be removed and the bran should not be refined by sifting. It should be well raised and noticeably salty. It should be well worked during kneading, and should be baked in the oven. This is the bread that to the physicians is properly prepared; it is the best of foods."

Maimonides,
Regimen of Health, Chapter I (1198)

El Pan de los Siete Cielos
The Bread of the Seven Heavens

Serves 6
Time: 1 hour

For the dough:

- 1 ⅓ cup (200 g) flour
- 1 ⅓ cup (200 g) semolina
- 1 ½ tsp salt
- 1 tbsp fresh yeast
- 1 cup (200 ml) lukewarm water

For the stuffing:

- 1 ⅓ cup (200 g) cheese (like feta)
- ¼ cup (60 g) olive oil
- ½ tsp salt
- 1 clove of garlic
- 5 leaves mint
- 1 strand thyme
- pomegranate (optional)
- honey (optional)

There is no medieval written source for this dish. This is not surprising, since there is no book that refers specifically and openly to Jewish culinary practices, due to fears of religious persecution. The dish originated in the Iberian Peninsula, and was later eaten in Salonika when the Jews migrated there after their official expulsion from Spain in 1492. It is traditionally prepared for Shavuot, also known as the "Feast of Weeks," or "Pentecost," a Jewish holiday marking the beginning of the wheat harvest and commemorating the sacred giving of the Torah to Moses and the people of Israel on Mount Sinai. There is a relation between bread and Heaven in the Torah: in Exodus (16, 4) God says to Moses, "I will rain down bread for you from the sky."

Even in the detailed Inquisition records of Spain, I did not find any information related to foods for Shavuot specifically. However, one interesting finding dates back to a trial in 1484 in the north of the country: it mentions that conversos *were keeping a fifty-day feast which they called "the giving of the Law." In another trial record from 1501, there is reference to a* converso *who was denounced for spending "all night, until the morning, cooking" to celebrate* Pascua del Espíritu Santo *(Shavuot or Pentecost). For Christians, this holiday is celebrated seven weeks after Easter. For Jews, Shavuot is celebrated seven weeks after Passover. Another relevant mention of Jewish recalcitrance appears in a trial from seventeenth-century Mexico, a Spanish colonial territory, where* conversos *were denounced for celebrating this holiday forty days after Passover.*

The significance of this bread's seven rings is interesting: some sources indicate it refers to the seven stages of holiness through which the soul passes when the body dies. But it could also symbolize the traditional seven-day waiting period after Passover, when Jews await the celebration of Shavuot and the giving of the Torah on Mount Sinai. Or maybe the rings represent the seven days during Passover when eating leavened bread is forbidden. The bread's shape likely represents Mount Sinai.

Even if there is no official historical source for this dish, I decided to recreate it and use cheese to stuff the bread, as cheese and other dairy products are traditionally consumed for Shavuot.

To make the filling, lightly crush the cheese in a bowl using a fork. Add the olive oil, crushed mint and garlic, thyme and salt. Leave the mixture in the fridge while you start on the dough.

Now start on the dough: dissolve the yeast in 3 generous tablespoons of lukewarm water. In a bowl, mix the flour, the semolina and the salt. Pour in the water and yeast. Knead for 10 to 15 minutes and cover with a towel. Let the dough rise for an hour.

Roll out the dough with a rolling pin until you have 1 hand wide and 5 hands long.

Distribute the filling along to the long edge, and roll up the dough.

Stretch the roll into a cylinder 2 cm in diameter (1 inch).

Now, grease your hands with olive oil and arrange the dough into a tall spiral, to create Mount Sinai.

Brush the bread with olive oil and sprinkle it with thyme and mint.

Line a roasting pan with baking paper, and leave the bread to rise for about 30 minutes.

Bake in a 375°F (190°C) oven for 30 minutes.

Mufakhkhar
The bagel from Syria

Makes 10
Time: 2 hours 30 minutes

- 3 ¼ cups (500 g) flour
- 1 tbsp (20 g) fresh yeast
- ⅔ cup (150 ml) lukewarm milk
- ⅓ cup (generous, 85 ml) lukewarm water
- 2 egg whites
- ½ tbsp (10 g) salt
- ½ tbsp (10 g) sugar
- egg wash
- seeds (poppy, sesame, nigella, linseed)

The Kitāb al-wuṣla ilā l-habīb fī wasf al-tayyabāt wa l-tīb *(Scents and Flavors the Banqueter Favors) is a cookery book compiled in Syria in the thirteenth century. It includes a section about* ka'ak *(small baked goods) "of several varieties," one of which I propose here, the* mufakhkhar. *The* Kitāb al-wuṣla *instructs us to "knead the dough [made with flour, milk and sourdough] with the spices [fenugreek and mastic, toasted anise, nigella seeds, coriander and sesame seeds] and leave to rise fully, then form rings. Fill a pan with water, and bring to a full boil. Put the rings on a dowel, lower them into the water, remove, and put on a tray." This thirteenth-century* mufakhkhar *recipe is probably the first for what is nowadays known as a* bagel.

Dissolve the yeast in 3 generous tablespoons of lukewarm water.

Mix the flour and the milk in a bowl. Pour in the rest of the water. Add the sugar, salt and egg whites.

Add the fresh yeast, dissolved.

Knead for 10 to 15 minutes.

Cover with a napkin and let the dough rise for an hour and a half.

Then, using your fists, punch as much air out of the dough as possible. Take it out of the container and knead it for two minutes. Leave to rest.

From a sheet of parchment paper, cut out 10 squares, 6 × 6 inches in size. Sprinkle each square very lightly with flour.

Divide the dough into 10 balls, and poke a hole in the middle of each. Put each ring on its piece of parchment paper. Cover and let the bagels rise for 20 minutes.

Turn on the oven at 410°F (210°C).

Bring some salted water to the boil in a large pan.

Take one of the pieces of parchment paper with its bagel on it. Turn it upside down into the water. Peel off the paper very carefully. Cook for 3 minutes on each side in the simmering water, two at a time if you have room.

Line a tray with parchment paper. Put the bagels on it and brush with egg wash. Sprinkle with your favorite seeds.

Bake for 15–20 minutes.

Empanaditas with spinach and cheese

Makes 20
Time: 1 hour 15 minutes

For the dough:

- 2 eggs
- 1 ¾ cup (280 g) flour
- ½ tsp (3 g) salt
- ⅓ cup (75 g) soft butter or margarine
- Egg wash

For the filling:

- 10.5 oz (300 g) fresh spinach
- 1 onion, chopped
- 1 clove of garlic, chopped
- 1 cup (150 g) *beyaz peynir* cheese (or feta)
- ¼ cup (50 ml) olive oil
- 1 handful chopped coriander
- 1 tsp salt
- 1 tsp pepper

With eggplant filling:

- 2 eggplants
- 1 garlic clove, chopped
  2 tbsp ground almonds (or breadcrumbs)
- 1 tsp salt
- 1 tsp pepper
- ½ tsp anise seeds

Here I propose an empanaditas *recipe with spinach and cheese stuffing from the* Kitāb al-ṭabīḫ [The Cookbook], *one of the books I analyzed as part of my doctoral research.*

To make the dough, beat the eggs and add the flour and the salt. Add the soft butter and mix all the ingredients together. Knead for 5 minutes until uniform and smooth. Put the dough in the fridge for 30 minutes.

Meanwhile, prepare the spinach filling. In a pan, fry the olive oil, garlic and onion for 3 minutes, until golden. Add the spinach and sauté for 5 minutes on a medium heat. Set aside to cool in a large bowl.

Once cool, add the cheese and the fresh coriander, and mix lightly. Cover the bowl and refrigerate for at least 20 minutes.

Roll out the dough thinly, to a tenth of an inch (a couple of millimeters) thickness. With a cookie cutter (2 in/5cm diameter), cut the dough into disks. Place them on a plate lined with parchment paper.

Put a spoonful of the filling in the middle of each disk. Moisten lightly the bottom of the disk with water and fold the top half over the bottom half. Flatten the edges, using the teeth of a fork to seal the dough. Once all the *empanaditas* are filled, put the plate in the fridge for at least 30 minutes.

Turn on the oven at 400°F (200°C). Arrange your cold *empanaditas* on a baking sheet lined with parchment paper. Brush them with egg wash, and once the oven is hot, bake for 15 minutes.

A delicious version of this recipe can be made with eggplant instead. Proceed as above, replacing the filling with this one:

Cook the eggplants in salted boiling water for 15 minutes. Strain them thoroughly in a colander. Hollow them out and put the flesh in a bowl, adding the garlic, salt, and pepper.

Once the eggplant mix is cold, add the ground almonds or breadcrumbs. Leave to rest for 30 minutes. Proceed as per the spinach and cheese *empanaditas*, and remember to add the anise seeds just after you have brushed them with egg wash, before baking.

In rabbinical writings, the term pashtida *refers to a dish akin to* empanadita. *In the Babylonian Talmud (Pesachim 74b and Rashi), this term is used in reference to a dish prepared and eaten on Shabbat, given its ease of transport and the possibility of consuming it at room temperature (having prepared it on the Friday).* Empanadas *are an integral part of Spain's culinary heritage; they are made of two layers of bread dough* (pan) *with a meat or vegetables and cheese stuffing.* Empanaditas *are a smaller version of this dish.* They *can be stuffed with any meat—or indeed any other filling, hidden within the dough. In the* Kitāb al-ṭabīḫ, *eggplants are used instead of hare meat (common in other contemporary cookbooks): since Muslims are not affected by this restriction, it is likely that this recipe was intended for Jews. Indeed, eggplant, with its dark color and dense texture, has often been used to simulate meat. The enclosed shape of the* empanaditas *and the use of eggplant made it possible to respect the rules of Kashrut and at the same time to deceive the Inquisition, which spied on the culinary practices of the Jews of Spain.*

After 1492, although Jews were banned from traveling across the Atlantic, some—cooks of aristocrats and churchmen, or even illegals—embarked for the New World and carried their cuisine from Sefarad with them, empanaditas *included. And as in Spain, this was used by the Inquisition tribunals of the new territories such as Mexico and Brazil to persecute* conversos.

Nowadays, non-Sephardic Spaniards eat the larger empanadas, often filled with pork or eel, while Sephardim all over the world continue to eat the smaller empanaditas, *with eggplant, fish, beef, or mutton.*

The making of *peot*: The *challah* from Spain in the thirteenth century

Serves 4
Time: 2 hours 25 minutes (20 min + 1 h + 30 min + 35 min)

For the dough:

- 5 eggs
- 3 cups flour (460 g)
- ¼ cup (87 g) extra fine semolina (or the same amount of flour if not using)
- 2 tbsp fresh yeast crushed (or 1 ½ tbsp active dry yeast, or 3 tbsp sourdough starter)
- 3 tbsp lukewarm water
- 2 saffron strands
- ¼ cup (60 g) olive oil
- ½ tsp salt
- 1 tsp orange blossom water
- 3 tbsp sugar (optional, for a sweeter flavor)
- egg wash

To drizzle:

- ⅛ cup (13 g) sugar
- ⅛ cup (20 g) honey
- ½ tsp pepper
- 1 tsp ground cinnamon
- ⅛ cup (25 g) butter (optional)
- dried lavender flowers

The challah braided bread, an icon of today's Ashkenazi Jewish cuisine, could have its first recorded recipe in Spain's first cookbook in the thirteenth century. Accompanying the Sephardic Jews who were expelled from the Iberian Peninsula in the fifteenth century, the challah began its long journey north and eastward, passing through Italy, to Eastern Europe. There it blended with the culinary practices of Ashkenazi Jews, who adopted it and gave it a home of permanence and survival not only at home but throughout the world.

This is the original recipe from the Kitāb al-ṭabīḫ *(in Arabic, translated by David Friedman):*

> Take what you will of white flour or of semolina, which is better in these things. Moisten it with hot water after sifting, and knead well, after adding some fine flour, leavening, and salt. Moisten it again and again until it has middling consistency. Then break into it, for each *ratl* of semolina, five eggs and a *dirham* of saffron, and beat all this very well, and put the dough in a dish, cover it and leave it to rise [...]. When it has risen, clean a frying pan and fill it with fresh oil, then put it on the fire. When it starts to boil, make braids of the leavened dough like hair-braids, of a handspan or less in size. Coat them with oil and throw them in the oil and fry them until they brown. When their cooking is done, arrange them on an earthenware plate and pour over them skimmed honey spiced with pepper, cinnamon, Chinese cinnamon, and lavender. Sprinkle it with ground sugar and present it.

In the original recipe, the challah is fried. Using the same recipe, I tried two cooking methods, fried and baked in the oven. Both crumbs are very similar, but my preference goes to the baked version. I also find that preparing the dough with flour works (rather than with both flour and semolina), but I shall leave this up to your preference in my version of the Kitāb al-ṭabīḫ *recipe below.*

In the bowl of a stand mixer, put the eggs, flour, semolina, saffron, olive oil, salt, orange blossom water, and sugar (if using). Mix slowly with the hook attachment for 30 seconds.

If you are using fresh yeast or active dry yeast, dissolve it in a small bowl with the lukewarm water for about 2 minutes first, then add it to the bowl of the stand mixer with the other ingredients.

If you are using a sourdough starter, put it directly in the bowl of the stand mixer with the other ingredients, and add the lukewarm water.

Mix all for at least 15 minutes on a medium speed (i.e. 2 or 3).

Grease another bowl lightly with oil. Transfer the dough out of the mixer bowl into the greased one, cover it with a plastic wrap and let the dough rise in a warm place for 1 hour.

Uncover the bowl. Grease your hands lightly and punch down the challah dough, to get some of the air out. Stir it in the stand mixer again for 5 minutes.

Put it back in the bowl, cover it again with plastic wrap and let it rise for another 30 minutes.

Then, punch the air out of the dough once again, before moving on to braiding.

You can braid your challah in a lot of different ways. The easiest one is with three braids.

Divide the dough in three balls of equal weight and diameter.

Roll them into 3 equally sized strands about 11 inches (30 cm) long. Their surface should be smooth, without grooves.

Lay the strands side by side and pinch the tops together. Start braiding as if you were braiding hair, placing the strands at each end alternatively in the middle between the other two strands. So, start with the right strand and put it between the middle and the left strands. Then, take the left strand put in between the middle and right strands, and so on. When you finish braiding, pinch the ends and fold under the loaf.

Place the braid on a lined tray and leave to rise in a warm place for 1 hour, covered with a kitchen towel. Preheat the oven to 330°F (170°C).

Lightly brush the challah dough with the egg wash and bake for 35 minutes until golden brown.

Meanwhile prepare the drizzle: melt the sugar, honey, and ground cinnamon (with the pepper and butter, if using) in a saucepan over medium heat. When the challah is baked, brush it with the syrup and let it cool. Decorate with the dried lavender flowers.

Challah is a term that has attracted a lot of interest from biblical times to the present day. Many scholars and lovers of Jewish cuisine have ventured into historical and culinary research—not always with sound findings—on the term's origins and on the dish itself. Stories of challah's history abound online and in cookery books, but there is little information actually drawn from historical sources.

I looked to what Iberian sources offer us, such as the Kitāb al-ṭabīḫ, *in Al-Andalus (southern Spain). In the manuscript it bears the name of* عمل الضفاير, *which means "the making [*عمل*] of braids [*الضفاير*]." The term "braids" corresponds to the word* ḍafair *in Arabic, which no other source or recipe from the same period mentions. What is interesting is that the Spanish translation of this recipe shows the word* guedejas *for "braids," and the closest translation of* guedejas *in Hebrew is the term* peot *(i.e. sidecurls). This recipe entitled "The making of braids" matches very closely with the preparation of challah braided bread.*

The two **challot** *on the left are fried (following the original thirteenth-century process) and the two on the right are baked in the oven.*

Baked muğabbana
Cheese pies

Serves 4
Time: 40 minutes

For the dough:

- 2 eggs
- 2 cups (300 g) flour
- ½ tsp (3 g) salt
- ⅓ cup (75 g) soft butter or margarine

For the stuffing:

- 1 cup (150 g) *beyaz peynir* cheese (or you can substitute feta)
- ½ tsp (3 g) salt
- 1 onion, chopped (optional)
- 1 garlic clove, chopped (optional)
- ¼ cup (50 g) olive oil (optional)

The term muğabbana *comes from the Arabic word* ğban, *which means "cheese," and from which the term* almojabana *(cheese buns) derives. But this "Recipe for oven-baked cheese pie" from the* Kitāb al-ṭabīẖ *is more similar to an* empanada, *as it has the shape of a small stuffed slipper. The recipe title calls it "Toledan," and we know that the Spanish city of Toledo had a significant Jewish community in the late Middle Ages. This dish took many shapes, and similar ones were prepared by the Sephardim of Turkey and of the Ottoman Empire.*

The original recipe only tells us to make the dough, spread it, and place just the right amount of crushed cheese in the middle, then fold the edges of the dough to completely cover the cheese. I will give a few more directions here.

First, mix all the dough ingredients and knead for 5 minutes. Cover and set aside in the fridge for 30 minutes.

For the stuffing, crumble the cheese and add the other ingredients into a bowl. Make sure not to overmix.

Roll out the dough quite thickly to about 3 mm (⅛ inch) and cut it into circles with a cookie cutter roughly the size of a fist.

Line a baking sheet with parchment paper and shape the *muğabbana* directly onto it. In the lower part of each circle, put a spoonful of cheese stuffing. Very lightly moisten the rim with water. Gently close by folding down the upper part. Press all around the dough with the teeth of a fork to close the *muğabbana*. Finally, make a small hole in the highest part of the *muğabbana* and sprinkle with anise seeds.

Bake in a hot 375°F (190°C) oven for 10–15 minutes.

Falafel
Simple chickpea croquettes

Makes 25
Time: 1 night (for the chickpeas) + 30 minutes

For the croquettes:

- 1 full cup (200 g) dry chickpeas
- ¼ tsp baking powder
- 2 tsp ground cumin
- 2 small garlic cloves, crushed
- ⅓ cup fresh coriander, chopped
- ⅓ cup parsley, chopped
- ½ tsp salt
- 1 tsp sesame seeds, white or golden (optional but recommended)
- neutral oil or olive oil for frying

For the sauce:

- 1 cup (225 g) heavy cream
- ⅛ to ¼ cup (30 g to 60 g) tahini
- juice of 1 lemon
- ½ tsp salt
- ½ tsp cumin seeds
- pomegranate seeds

This is one of the twelve chickpea recipes offered in the Kitāb al-ṭabīḫ, *and it is a very intriguing one. It explains how to mince the chickpeas, add yeast, eggs, and spices, and how to shape and fry the croquettes, which are served with a sauce. This resembles clearly the recipe for falafel, consumed in the Middle East by Jews and many others. This culinary discovery of what is probably the first falafel recipe written in a cookbook in the Muslim West adds an interesting finding to the debate on the geographical and ethnic origin of this emblematic dish of the Middle Eastern culinary culture.*

Soak the chickpeas in water overnight, then dry them with a paper towel.

Chop the coriander and parsley very finely, but make sure the herbs are dry: there must be no water, or you will not be able to form the croquettes and they will crumble when frying. Add the chopped garlic cloves, baking powder, cumin, salt, and sesame seeds (if using). Refrigerate for 1 hour.

Shape the croquettes with a falafel maker, or, with the help of two spoons, make balls the size of a golf ball and flatten them softly. Fry them in oil at medium-hot temperature. Do not move the croquettes for the first 2 or 3 minutes, otherwise they will crumble. Then, gently turn them over.

Take the croquettes out and put them on a paper towel.

Prepare the sauce by mixing all the ingredients. Adjust the tahini and lemon juice depending on how thick you like it. Serve with the falafel.

Matza
Unleavened bread

Makes 4
Time: 18 minutes

- 1 ⅛ cup (170 g) flour
- ½ cup (100 ml) water

Matza is one of the few the dishes in this book that are exclusively Jewish. This unleavened, yeast-free bread, prepared by Jews for the feast of Passover—Pesach—is linked to the liturgical and cultural practices of Judaism. Passover, along with Yom Kippur, is the most celebrated Jewish holiday. It commemorates the Exodus and liberation from slavery of the Jews from Egypt: since they had to flee quickly, the Torah tells that their bread could not rise and had to be eaten unleavened. It is in remembrance of this that matza is eaten during the two Seder *ritual meals and the week of Passover. Thus, this was one of the dishes often used to denounce crypto-Jews during the Inquisition: for example, trial records from 1488 tell us of a Diego García Costello, from Spain, who would go door to door looking for* pan canceño *(unleavened bread) for Passover. Later, in Mexico in 1642, a Beatriz Enríquez, although herself a* conversa, *described to the inquisitors how her mother Blanca took great care in preparing matza, with the same simple ingredients as were used among Jews in Spain in other trial records: flour, water, no salt, no yeast.*

Preheat your cast iron slab, or your oven, ideally to 600°F (315°C) or as hot as your oven goes. Put parchment paper in a baking sheet. Take a rolling pin and a fork, and keep them close to you.

Mix together the water and the flour, and knead the dough for 5 minutes.

Cut the dough into 4 pieces and roll them into balls. Each ball should fit in the palm of your hand.

Take the rolling pin (or your hands) and spread each ball as a very thin layer of dough: you can make one ball a minute (6 inches diameter). According to the liturgy, for the matza to be kosher for Passover, the preparation should not be longer than 18 minutes from beginning to end.

Put the matza over the parchment paper on the baking sheet, and prick it with the fork.

Bake for 2 and a half minutes on one side and 30 seconds on the other side.

Calentita
Chickpea flour cake

Serves 8
Time: 24 hours + 40 minutes

- 2 cups (250 g) chickpea flour
- 4 ¼ cups (850 ml) water
- ½ cup (100 g) olive oil
- 1 tsp salt
- 2 tsp cumin
- 1 tsp paprika
- 2 eggs (for a creamier result)

In Gibraltar, where Jews and Muslims continue to live together as they have for many generations, a culinary festival called Calentita *is organized every year at the beginning of July. "Calentita" is the most commonly Arabic translation for the dish* chalawen. *The* calentita *became one of the culinary symbols of Gibraltar, to such an extent that special chickpea flour is milled in the United Kingdom and imported to Gibraltar for this occasion. The name* calentita *(or* calentica*) comes from the Spanish* caliente, *meaning "hot." This festival reminds us of the coexistence of Jewish and Muslim communities, living side by side now as they did in the past.*

Healthy, dairy-free, flourless and unusual, calentita *is a truly original dish for Passover that will give a North African flavor to your menu.*

Mix the chickpea flour, water, olive oil, salt and eggs (if using) together in a bowl and refrigerate for 24 hours.

Preheat the oven at 428°F (220°C).

Pour the mixture into a greased square pie pan and bake for 25 minutes.

Serve hot or lukewarm, cut into thin slices or small squares, and sprinkled with cumin, paprika, and salt.

Corn *tortillas*
A Passover Mexican crypto-Jewish dish

Serves 4
Time: 1 hour

Dough:

- 2 cups (300 g) corn flour/ masa harina (nixtamalized)
- 1 ½ tsp salt
- 1 ⅓ cup (260 ml) hot water
- 1 tsp olive oil

Fish and sauce:

- ¼ cup (50 g) olive oil
- 2 chopped cloves of garlic
- ½ lb (220 g) fresh white fish
- 2 very thinly sliced red onions
- 2 tbsp chopped fresh cilantro
- ½ tsp black pepper
- 2 tbsp finely chopped chives
- juice of 1 lime
- 1 tsp salt

Corn tortillas are undeniably linked to the culinary heritage of Mexico, since they were already prepared in pre-Columbian times. As we know, adaptability is inherent to Jewish culture, both for the survival of its culture and its people. Conversos *had been replacing wheat flour with chestnut flour when making Passover matza (wheat being one of the grains not eaten at Passover), as reported in the trials of the Portuguese Inquisition; the same applies to corn flour in the preparation of tortillas. In the middle of the seventeenth century in Mexico, Salomón de Machorro (aka Juan de León, famous for his travels and knowledge of Judaism) was denounced for having consumed corn tortillas with fish and vegetables with his friends for Passover.*

To make the dough, mix together corn flour and salt in a large bowl. Add the olive oil and the hot water.

Mix the preparation with a spoon until all the water is absorbed.

Make balls the size of a golf ball. Leave them to rest on a plate for 20 minutes, covered so they do not dry. Now to flatten and cook the tortillas, you can use a tortilla press if you have one: remember to put the dough ball between two pieces of parchment paper so it does not stick to the press; place it in the center of the bottom part of the press, then open it and carefully, with the palm of your hand, remove the tortilla from the parchment sheet. If you don't have a tortilla press, you can use the bottom of a heavy saucepan and press down hard. Again, do not forget the parchment paper!

Cook in a preheated (medium-high heat) nonstick skillet for 20 seconds. Then flip the tortilla over and cook the other side for 20 seconds more. Repeat the operation once more until the tortilla has golden-brown marks.

Keep the tortillas in a plastic bag, not completely closed, while you make the filling.

Put olive oil, red onions, and garlic in a frying pan. Cook for 5 minutes on medium heat until golden.

Add the fresh fish cut into pieces and pour in the fresh lime juice. Add salt and black pepper. Cover the frying pan and cook on a low heat for 5 minutes.

Then, sprinkle with the chopped fresh cilantro and chives.

Now fill the corn tortillas with the delicious fish and its lime juice.

VOUS
DE
PRODUIT EN FRANCE

DEUR VIENNE
CHER AFIN
CTER LES
BARRIÈRES
Marcel
100% PORTUGAL
ORANGE
PORTUGAL
CA

VEGETABLES AND EGGS

Maimonides's food at the end of his life.

"Many times I had chicken soup and slept, and sometimes I cooked five to six eggs and ate their yolks with a little sugar cane and salt, and sometimes I ate a little pistachio and raisins without pits, and almonds and *panis*, and I drank a sugar and honey drink."

Maimonides,
The Book of Asthma, Chapter VI (late twelfth century).

Güesmo
A Swiss chard dish

Serves 4
Time: 40 minutes

For the bread:

- 1 tbsp of olive oil
- ¼ tsp of salt
- ½ clove of garlic, chopped
- 4 thick slices of bread

For the güesmo:

- ⅛ cup (30 g) olive oil
- 2 cloves of garlic, chopped
- 2 onions, sliced
- ½ tsp black pepper
- 2 tsp sugar
- 7 oz (200 g) Swiss chard
- ½ tsp of salt
- ½ tsp ground cumin
- 4 tsp grated cheese (like Swiss or feta)
- 2 tsp pine nuts
- salt

Here is a historical and healthy dish called güesmo, *made traditionally in celebration of* Tu Bishvat, *or "The New Year of the Trees": the day occurs on the 15th of Shevat, and fruit, vegetables, and nuts are traditionally eaten to evoke the renewal of leaves and trees.*

Preheat the oven to 425°F (220°C).

Mix together 1 tbsp of olive oil, ¼ tsp of salt and ½ clove of chopped garlic in a bowl.

Brush the slices of bread with this mixture on both sides. Put them on a baking sheet and bake them for 4 minutes until crisp. Set aside.

For the *güesmo*:

Wash the chard and remove the stems, keeping the green leaves only. Immerse the leaves in boiling salted water for 6 minutes. Drain and rinse with cold water to keep them green, and squeeze them to remove all the water.

Heat the ⅛ cup of oil in a pan. Add the chopped garlic cloves, the 2 onions very thinly sliced, and the black pepper. Cook for 5 minutes until it is light brown. Sprinkle with sugar.

Add the chard leaves, ½ tsp of salt, and the ground cumin, and cook on a low heat for 5 minutes.

Take the toasted slices of bread. Put the swiss chard mixture onto the bread.

Sprinkle on the grated cheese and the pine nuts. Toast in the oven for 2 minutes. Be careful not to burn it.

To make some good-looking individual portions you can use a round cookie cutter.

I love Swiss chard. It is a tasty alternative to spinach and the size and shape of its leaves offer many fancy possibilities for creative culinary delights. Of Mediterranean origin, Swiss chard was mentioned by Hippocrates in Diaita *(*Regimen in Health, *II, 54, 4) as early as 400 BCE. The Talmud also mentions that consuming it is recommended*

to ensure good health. Used in Spain since the Middle Ages, it was one of the ingredients associated with the culinary customs of the conversos*: records from fifteenth-century Toledo, Spain, talk about a dish prepared by* conversos *with Swiss chard, cumin, onions, black pepper, caraway, chickpeas, broad beans, eggplant, and fat meat (like mutton or lamb), cooked overnight. The amazing smell it emanated was called* güesmo*. Similarly, in northern Spain at the beginning of the sixteenth century, a dish with Swiss chard, cheese, and breadcrumbs was prepared for Shivah (a formal seven-day period of mourning) by a daughter after her father died. There are also records of another Swiss chard dish from the Spanish Middle Ages, made with boiled and fried leaves, onions, breadcrumbs, and spices, and usually cooked on Friday nights for Shabbat.*

Huebos hammados
Red hard-boiled eggs

Serves 6 pieces
Time: 6 hours

- 6 eggs
- red onion peel (enough to cover all eggs completely).
- ½ cup (100 ml) white vinegar

Known nowadays as huevos haminados, *this dish has been part of the culinary practices of Jews and Sephardim of Spain at least since the fifteenth century. From the word "ham" which means "hot" in Hebrew, these are in fact hard-boiled eggs cooked for a very long time, so that the white turns red-brown and the yolk darkens. Eggs were part of the daily diet for everyone in the Middle Ages, but Jews were seemingly particularly fond of their symbolic meaning (from the cycle of life, to servitude, mourning, and even joy). Pedro Martines, a clothier from the Spanish city of Soria, was denounced in 1490 for consuming milk and red eggs during Lent (which corresponded to Passover). This is also one of the reasons why Alvaro de Luna was tried on June 5, 1505 in the city of Almazán: witness María de Fernando had seen him eat red eggs on Fridays and during Lent.*

Wash the eggs with vinegar: this will allow the color to fix better on the shell and dye the egg whites more easily.

Put the red onion peel into a saucepan and place the fresh eggs on top. Cover them with more peel.

Add the white vinegar, then cover with boiling water.

Cook over a very low heat for six hours.

Cut in half and sprinkle with cumin and salt. You can pour 1 tsp olive oil over them if you like, and enjoy with lettuce and cheese.

Eggplant *almodrote*
Eggplant, garlic, and cheese dip

Serves 4
Time: 30 minutes

- 2 medium eggplants
- 1 small onion, sliced
- 1 garlic clove
- 3 tbsp olive oil
- 1 ½ tsp salt
- 2 tsp vinegar
- ½ cup (50 g) grated hard cheese (like Parmesan)

In the Kitāb al-ṭabīḫ *there is a recipe called "Recipe for boiled eggplant," which strongly resembles a dish consumed today in northern Spain called* almodrote. *It also appears in another cookbook written in southeastern Spain (Murcia) in the thirteenth century, where it is called the "other dish": the* Fuḍālat al-ḫiwān. *Additionally, the* Sent Soví *cookbook, written in Catalan in the fourteenth century under Christian rule, contains both a version of this recipe without eggplant (only the garlic and cheese sauce), bearing the Catalan name of* almadroc, *and one called* albergínies, *which actually corresponds to the* almodrote *with eggplant dish that Sephardic communities eat today. These findings suggest a Jewish culinary influence in fourteenth-century Catalan cuisine, and we know that the recipe was spread by Sephardic Jews to Morocco as well. In etymological terms,* almodrote *is a Hispano-Arabic word deriving from the term* almaṭrúq, *which could be translated as "that which is crushed"—*maṭrūq *meaning "crushed" in classical Arabic (*majado *in Spanish). Spanish lexicographer Covarrubias indicates that the word also designated a sauce used for seasoning eggplants, made of ingredients such as oil, cheese, and garlic.*

I personally named this recipe almodrote *because it closely matches the dish still made today with mashed eggplant, oil, cheese, and garlic.*

Wash the eggplants, prick them with a fork, and cook them for 20 minutes in salted water. If the eggplants rise to the surface, put a plate on top of the pot. In another pan, do the same with the onion.

Once the eggplant and onion are cooked, take them out and remove as much water as possible. Gently remove the skin from the eggplants and put the flesh in a bowl. Add the cooked onion. Mash everything quickly with a fork and set aside for 5 minutes. Discard any liquid.

Add the very thinly chopped garlic, olive oil, salt, and vinegar.

Sprinkle with cheese and mix very lightly.

You can eat it on toast with a trickle of olive oil.

Acelgas con garbanzos
Swiss chard stew with chickpeas

Serves 4
Time: 30 minutes

- 1 ½ cup (200 g) cooked chickpeas
- 1 bunch Swiss chard
- ⅛ cup (25 g) olive oil
- 2 garlic cloves, chopped
- ½ pound (220 g) beef steak (optional)
- 3 very thinly sliced onions
- 1 tsp black pepper
- 1 tsp salt
- 1 handful chopped cilantro

Here are two of the ingredients frequently used in adefina *recipes prepared by Sephardic crypto-Jews for Shabbat (more on this later): in an Inquisition trial record from July 13, 1590, we learn that Catalina Albarez, a* conversa, *prepared a dish with meat (from which she had carefully removed the fat), Swiss chard, and chickpeas.*

The recipe below is the first one that my grandmother Ana Guillen Palma taught me.

Wash the Swiss chard. Separate the stems and leaves and peel the white stems with the vegetable peeler. Cut sections the width of a finger. Take the leaves and remove the larger white veins. Cook the leaves in salted boiling water for 10 minutes. Take them out of the water and squeeze them in a drainer so the water comes out. Cook the white stems in the same way, then set them aside.

Put the olive oil, onions, garlic, salt, and pepper into a frying pan. If using meat, add it to the pan now, cut into slices. Add the cooked chickpeas and cook for 5 minutes on a medium heat.

Add the Swiss chard leaves and the stems. Cover the frying pan and cook at low heat for 5 more minutes.

Sprinkle with the chopped cilantro and serve.

EGGPLANTS

Eggplants are the very essence of Sephardi cuisine. Unknown to the Greeks and Romans, what the Swedish eighteenth-century naturalist *Linnaeus* classified as *Solanum melongena L.* was cultivated by the Mesopotamians (in the Fertile Crescent, present-day Iraq) at the beginning of the Christian era. Coming from the Indian subcontinent, the eggplant traveled to the Arabian Peninsula and settled in Spain in the tenth century. The spread of this *Solanacea* to the European West started in Italy in the fifteenth century. The conquest of the New World would subsequently transport the eggplant to Central America, Brazil, and North America in the nineteenth century.

Eggplants often failed to win unanimous support. In the *Regimen of Health* (1198), Maimonides advises against their consumption, writing that it is bad for men. It was also named "malum insanum" by fifteenth-century humanist Barbarus.

An analysis of cookbooks written under Christian domination, as well as numerous literary and legal sources, suggests eggplants were often consumed by Sephardic Jews. This generated a negative and often satirical culinary association, used to ridicule and denounce *conversos*; a fact reflecting a way of thinking that went much further than food criticism. This is evidenced by the words of Peregrino Artusi, nineteenth-century Italian scholar, gastronome, and author of *La Scienza in Cucina e Arte di Mangiar Bene* (1892), who wrote that in the early 1800s "eggplants were almost impossible to find in the Florence market; they were despised, because they were identified as Jewish food."

Eggplant *isfīriyā* croquettes

Makes 12
Time: 1 hour

For the béchamel:

- ¼ cup (50 g) butter
- ½ cup (60 g) flour
- ¾ cup (180 ml) milk
- 1 tsp salt

For the croquettes:

- 1 big eggplant (234 g/8 oz)
- 1 tbsp wine vinegar
- 1 garlic clove
- ½ tsp cumin powder
- ¼ cup (50 g) grated cheese
- ¼ cup (20 g) fresh coriander (optional)
- ½ tsp salt
- ½ tsp black pepper
- 1 cup (120 g) fine breadcrumbs
- 1 egg
- olive oil or neutral oil for frying

This recipe is not explicitly defined as Jewish: in the Kitāb al-ṭabīḫ, *it is one of the many preparations made with eggplants. It testifies to the taste and culinary preferences of the Jews and also Muslims, but likely not Christians: the almost complete absence of eggplants in the cookbooks of Spain under Christian domination testifies to the will of the new leaders to erase the eating habits of the Semitic peoples from the culinary heritage of Spain.*

The recipe presented here is still a snack consumed by everyone regardless of their religious beliefs, both in Andalusia and in some countries where the Sephardim live today.

To prepare the béchamel, melt the butter in a saucepan. Then, add the flour and mix quickly.

Add the milk little by little and then the salt. The mixture must be thick. Set aside and once cooled put in the fridge for 1 hour until it firms up.

Meanwhile, prepare the eggplants: slice and boil them in salted water and wine vinegar for 20 minutes.

Drain them and let them cool. Squeeze them to extract all the liquid.

Chop two cloves of garlic and the coriander. Add to a bowl with cumin, salt, and black pepper.

Mash the eggplant and add to the bowl.

Add the grated cheese and mix everything together. Pour in the bechamel. Cover the preparation and put it in the freezer for 1 hour.

Pour the oil into a frying pan—it should be one finger deep (1 cm).

Beat 1 egg in a bowl and prepare the breadcrumbs on a plate.

Take a tablespoon of the croquette mix, without trying to roll it or shape it.

Coat the mix with the beaten egg, and then in the breadcrumbs, coating all sides. Now, you can shape it into a croquette. Repeat with the rest of the mixture.

Fry the croquettes in medium-hot oil. Do not touch them for the first 2 minutes, then turn to cook all sides.

Put them on a paper towel to dry and serve hot.

Almoronía
Eggplant and meatballs

Serves 2
Time: 1 hour

- 2 eggplants
- 4.5 oz (130 g) chopped lamb cutlet without bone
- 1 large onion, chopped
- ½ cup (100 g) olive oil
- 1 tsp vinegar
- 3 tsp salt
- 1 tsp black pepper
- ½ cup (30 g) fresh coriander, chopped
- 1 tsp ginger
- 1 tsp cumin
- ½ tsp cinnamon
- 3 saffron strands
- ½ cup neutral oil for frying
- 1 tbsp sugar (or honey)
- ⅓ cup (50 g) chopped almonds

For the meatballs:

- 10.5 oz (300 g) ground fat lamb (or beef)
- ½ cup (30 g) fresh coriander, chopped
- 1 tsp salt
- 1 tsp black pepper

Almoronía *is a dish deeply ingrained in the culinary heritage of the Sephardic Jews of Morocco. In the* Kitāb al-ṭabīẖ*, there are four recipes titled* būrāniyya*,* alburānya *or* burānya*. In the late sixteenth century in the Spanish city of Granada, the dish "boronia" was recognized and denounced as a Jewish dish. Nowadays, non-Sephardim make* alboronía *(as every Spaniard knows it) with tomatoes, peppers, onions, zucchini, and eggplant cooked in olive oil. What is interesting, however, is that the* Kitāb al-ṭabīẖ *recipe for* burānya *is preserved today by Moroccan Jews, who are the only ones still preparing it as it appears here, with meat and eggplant, without peppers or tomatoes. Moroccan Jews consume the dish before starting (or after) the fast of Yom Kippur. Here is a recipe for* almoronía *in which the ingredients and method of preparation remain almost unchanged from the original.*

Chop the lamb in very small pieces and put it in a pot with olive oil, salt, chopped onion, black pepper, vinegar, coriander, ginger, cumin, saffron, and cinnamon.

Add the vinegar and cook for 5 minutes. Keep covered and warm.

Cut the eggplants into thick slices and boil in salted water for 4 minutes. Dry the slices on a paper towel.

Heat the oil in a frying pan. Fry the eggplant slices on one side for 3 minutes, then sprinkle with sugar, and fry the other side. Set aside.

Mix together the ground lamb, chopped coriander, salt, and pepper. Form small meatballs rolling them in your hands and fry them for 3–4 minutes in the same frying pan used to fry the eggplant (add some oil if necessary). Set aside.

Arrange a layer of fried eggplant on a plate. Then add a layer of meat, and another of eggplant on top. Finally, add the meatballs sprinkled with chopped almonds.

Warm up in the oven for 10 minutes at 400°F (200°C) before serving.

Sweet fried eggplants to break the fast

Serves 4
Time: 30 minutes

- 2 medium eggplants
- 2 tsp salt
- ½ cup (100 g) olive oil for frying
- 1 tsp salt
- ⅛ cup (20 g) honey

Eggplants and Sephardim have become a true culinary love story. There are so many eggplant dishes consumed by Sephardic Jews from Spain, Portugal, Turkey, Morocco, and more, that a single book would not be enough to present them. One interesting story about this is from Juan de León (aka Salomón Machorro): in 1646, while imprisoned in Mexico, he would ask the jailers for "two honeyed dishes" to break the fast, which he observed with his fellow prisoner Francisco Botello on Mondays, Wednesdays, and Fridays. This would have been an eggplant-based dish very similar to the one below.

Nowadays, eggplant dishes are traditionally prepared to break the fast in the Jewish communities: here I propose a sweet dish I particularly like and which is still eaten in Andalusia.

Wash the eggplants. Cut them into slices a finger wide. Sprinkle them with salt and let them drain for 20 minutes.

Pour the olive oil into a frying pan and heat over medium-high heat.

Coat the eggplants in the flour and tap them on the edge of a plate (not with your fingers) to remove excess. Place the eggplant slices in the pan without overlapping them. Fry for 5 minutes over medium heat without moving them so that they brown. Gently turn them over and cook for 5 minutes on the other side.

Place the fried slices on a large plate. Add a little salt if necessary and pour a drizzle of honey over it.

Caçuelas Eggplants with saffron and Swiss chard for a *converso* wedding

Serves 4
Time: 1 hour

- 3 medium eggplants
- 1 bunch Swiss chard
- ½ cup (100 g) olive oil
- 2 sliced onions
- 2 garlic cloves
- 3 saffron strands
- ½ tsp salt
- ½ tsp black pepper
- meatballs/*albóndigas* (optional)

One of the characteristics of eggplant is that it can be eaten cold. The culinary practices of the Jewish conversos *during the Inquisition period testify to this. Indeed, several families were accused by the court of the Inquisition of Toledo for having consumed "cold eggplant pots" called "caçuelas" for their Shabbat lunch, which they had prepared the day before. However, evidence of the consumption of these eggplant stews by Sephardic Jews from Spain is also found in Spanish literature. In the* Cancionero del siglo XV *there is a "copla" composed of satirical verses, intended for the* converso *Pedro González, and written by Rodrigo de Cota, also a* converso. *The verses mention Jewish dishes at Christian banquets, and, in particular, at the wedding of the grandson of Diego Aria-Dávila (who is mentioned in the trials of the Inquisition): a wedding between a* converso *bridegroom and a Christian bride where the absence of pork and fish without scales has been compensated by eggplants. The verses are: "At the aljama's wedding / We ate nothing thorny / Nor fish without scales / But as soon as the husband could / Lots of eggplants / And saffron with chard." The "aljama," an Arabic term used in Christian Spain to designate the Jewish (but sometimes Muslim) quarter, not only tells us where the celebration happened, but it also highlights that the celebration was a Jewish wedding. The verses emphasize the respect of this family for the Kashrut dietary laws, and imply that Jews "tricked" the people around them as they returned to eating their traditional food (eggplants, chard, etc.) as soon as they were safe from prying eyes ("as soon as the husband could").*

Wash the eggplants and cut them into slices as wide as a finger.

Wash the Swiss chard. Separate the stems and leaves. Cut the stems so you have sections as wide as a finger. Take the large green leaves and remove the larger veins of the leaf. Put the leaves and the stems in salted boiling water and cook for 15 minutes. Take them out of the water and put them in a colander. Squeeze them so that the water comes out.

Pour the olive oil in a frying pan, add the sliced onions, chopped garlic, salt, pepper, and saffron. Cook for 5 minutes on medium heat.

Then, put down the eggplant slices in the frying pan so as to form one layer only, not overlapping. Then, make the second layer with the cooked chard. Cover the pan and cook at low heat for 10-15 minutes more. Wait 10 minutes and turn the dish upside down onto a plate.

This dish goes perfectly with meatballs (*albóndigas*), either as a side or added between the chard and the eggplants.

THE EXPLICITLY JEWISH DISHES

between the Western cookbook *Kitāb al-ṭabīẖ* and the Eastern cookbook *Kitāb al-waṣf al-aṭ'ima al-mu'tāda*

February 14, 1604. This is the date of the earliest copy we have of the first Western Muslim cookbook, the *Kitāb al-ṭabīẖ*, presenting recipes and culinary practices dating back to the twelfth and thirteenth century. What we call the Muslim West essentially identifies the Iberian Peninsula of the Middle Ages, so studying the cuisine of this vast territory entails analyzing eating and culinary habits over a period of almost eight centuries. It can certainly be qualified as "intercultural," given the coexistence and intermingling of different culinary cultures in the same space and at the same time. In the second century, three culinary traditions coexisted in the Iberian Peninsula: Iberian, Celtic, and Roman and pan-Mediterranean. From the fifth century, we see the addition of the Visigoth tradition. Finally, in 711 AD, the arrival of Muslims in the Iberian territory introduced a new culture and cuisine. All the while, Jews and Christians lived together in the Iberian Peninsula, with their separate dietary practices reflecting their respective beliefs. Historians generally agree that the cultural pinnacle of the Muslim West was between the ninth and eleventh centuries, when the sharing of knowledge and culture between different groups reached its peak. However, the differences between Jewish, Christian, and Muslim communities later emerged, and the cultural exchange—also from a culinary point of view—drastically diminished. It is in this context that the first cookbook of the Muslim West was written, in Arabic. The *Kitāb al-ṭabīẖ* consists of more than half a thousand very diverse recipes, witness to the multicultural cuisine of Al-Andalus. But only six of the recipes are explicitly called Jewish.

As for the Middle East, we know it had a vast Jewish community during the Middle Ages. But where are the traces of its cuisine? No known author is Jewish, which is surprising considering the large number of Jewish doctors of this period in the fertile crescent. In the myriad Eastern Muslim cookbooks of the Middle Ages, the only one to include dishes explicitly designated as Jewish is the *Kitāb al-waṣf al-aṭ'ima al-mu'tāda* [The Description of Familiar Foods], an anonymous cookbook written in Cairo (1373). The recipe is *Makābīb la'nūhā a l-Yahūd*, "the meatballs *cursed* by the Jews." This telling attribute speaks volumes about the contemporary social outlook towards Jews in the region. The second recipe—which in fact is the same recipe as the first one—to mention the word "Jew" in the title does not appear until the seventeenth-eighteenth century. After almost 400 years, the first meatball recipe has lost the word "cursed" and now uses another type of meat. It is entitled *Makābib al-Yahūd*, "Meatballs of the Jews."

"A Jewish dish of chicken," with stuffing

Serves 4
Time: 1 hour 15 minutes

- 1 whole small chicken with its giblets
- ¼ cup (36 g) chopped walnuts
- ¼ cup (30 g) breadcrumbs
- ⅛ cup (18 g) flour
- 1 tbsp salt
- ¼ cup (30 g) chopped fennel (green and white parts)
- 1 handful fresh cilantro
- 3 small eggs
- 1 tbsp water
- ¾ cup (150 g) olive oil
- 2 tbsp rue
- 2 tbsp mint leaves
- 2 tbsp roasted chopped walnuts

Here is the first of the Jewish recipes from the Muslim West. It dates from the thirteenth century and can be found in the Kitāb al-ṭabīẖ. *The title of the recipe in Arabic is* لون من فروج يهوديى, *which means "A **Jewish** dish of Chicken."*

Chop the chicken giblets and mix with walnuts, breadcrumbs, flour, salt, fennel, cilantro, eggs, and water.

Take the chicken and put in a pot with olive oil. Brown it on all sides.

Remove the chicken, and add the stuffing to the same pot. Cook for 5 minutes while stirring. Set aside.

Add the chicken into the pot again with ¼ cup of olive oil or more. Cover and cook over low-medium heat for 45 minutes.

Finally, put the cooked chicken in a dish and dress with the stuffing around it. Sprinkle the dish with chopped fennel, chopped rue, mint leaves, and toasted walnuts.

"A Jewish dish of chicken"

Serves 4
Time: 1 hour 30 minutes

- 1 small chicken (separate legs, wings, and neck) + liver
- 1 tsp cumin
- 1 tsp powdered ginger
- 2 onions
- 2 tbsp pine nuts
- 1 ½ cups (300 g) olive oil
- ½ cup (120 g) vinegar
- 1 handful fresh coriander
- 3 etrog leaves (or lemon tree leaves)
- 1 whole fennel, chopped
- 1 tbsp salt
- 2 tsp black pepper
- 6 eggs
- ½ cup (60 g) breadcrumbs
- ¼ cup (35 g) flour

For the sauce:

- ¼ cup (50 g) olive oil
- ⅛ cup (25 g) rose water
- 1 tbsp vinegar
- ¼ cup (45 g) onions, chopped
- 2 tsp ground cumin
- 2 tsp ground ginger
- 1 tbsp fresh cilantro, chopped
- 1 tsp salt

For the presentation:

- 3 hard-boiled yolks
- 2 tsp cumin seeds
- ½ tsp salt

This is the second explicitly Jewish recipe of the Kitāb al-ṭabīḫ. *One of the peculiarities is that in preparing the chicken, the legs, wings, and neck are cut and covered with salt. This was a way to boost the evacuation of blood from the meat.*

Put the cut chicken in a pot. Add the cumin and ginger. Peel the onions and put them in a blender at full power. Put the onion puree in the pot and add whole pine nuts, 1 cup oil, ¼ cup vinegar, mashed green coriander, etrog leaves (or lemon leaves), chopped fennel, salt, and black pepper. Cover and cook for 20 minutes over medium heat.

Take a bowl and beat 3 eggs. Add the breadcrumbs and the flour. Mix all together. Add this mixture to the cooked chicken.

Add the pounded chicken liver, cover, and cook for another 10 minutes.

Transfer all to an ovenproof dish (if the pot is not).

In another bowl, mix ¼ cup vinegar with 3 beaten eggs and ½ cup olive oil. Use this to coat the chicken and grill in a hot oven at 400°F (200°C) for 5 minutes.

Prepare the sauce mixing oil, rose water, vinegar, chopped onions, cumin, ginger, chopped cilantro, and salt.

Finally, put the chicken in a large plate and pour the sauce over it.

Decorate with chopped hard-boiled egg yolks, cumin seeds, and salt.

"Jewish partridge," stuffed

Serves 4
Time: 1 hour 30 minutes

- 1 whole partridge + giblets
- 1 pound (450 g) coarse salt
- 1 tbsp chopped almonds
- 1 tbsp chopped pine nuts
- 1 tbsp vinegar
- ¼ cup (50 g) olive oil
- 1 tbsp fresh coriander, very finely chopped
- ½ tsp black pepper
- 1 short cinnamon stick
- 6 beaten eggs
- 6 whole hard-boiled egg yolks
- 5 etrog (or lemon) leaves
- 5 mint leaves
- ½ tbsp chopped pistachios
- ½ tbsp chopped almonds
- ½ tbsp chopped toasted pine nuts
- ½ tsp black pepper
- ½ tsp cinnamon powder
- ½ tsp sugar

This is the third explicitly Jewish recipe, حجلة يهودية *in the* Kitāb al-ṭabīḫ. *The partridge appears in biblical sources: in the Chumash (Leviticus/ Vayikra), it is written that "Unlike kosher animals and fish, whose identification is based on physical characteristics, the identity of authorized birds is very fuzzy. The Torah lists twenty-five species of non-kosher birds, which means that all others are kosher." The partridge does not appear on this list. Al-Rāzī (d. 925 or 935) recognizes the benefits of its consumption and Maimonides also mentions it. In this recipe as well the meat is salted before cooking. The method is particularly interesting: the partridge is placed in a pot whose lid must be sealed with dough, so that nothing can be added to it—this is typical of Shabbat cooking. Also interesting are the instructions that the egg yolks should be arranged in a star shape to decorate the dish: the star, which also appears in the next recipe, is reminiscent of the Star of David. Arranging eggs in star shape is also mentioned in the trials of the Inquisition of the city of Teruel (northern Spain), where conversos "estrellaban" (from the word "estrella" which means "star") eggs in a frying pan.*

Pluck the whole partridge and cover it with the coarse salt. Let stand for 15 minutes and rinse it.

Chop the giblets and mix with almonds, pine nuts, vinegar, oil, coriander juice, pepper, cinnamon, and 2 beaten eggs. Set aside.

Hard-boil 2 eggs, and stuff the partridge with them.

Place the stuffed partridge, with all the ingredients, in a pot [the original recipe states that the pot must be new]. Add etrog (or lemon) and mint, and break 2 eggs on top of the partridge.

Put a lid on the pot and seal it with dough made from flour and water (or put a damp cloth around it). [The original recipe instructs us to cover the pot with another copper pot full of embers (to brown the top), and then turn it over to cook the bottom].

Cook the dish over a medium heat for 20 minutes.

Take off the lid and place the pot under a hot grill for 5 minutes.

Place the cooked partridge in a dish with the stuffing all around. Then, to garnish, place 6 whole hard-boiled egg yolks around the partridge to draw a star.

Sprinkle it with pepper, cinnamon, and sugar. If you like, add pistachios, almonds, and toasted pine nuts on top.

“A Jewish dish of partridge”

Serves 4
Time: 1 hour

- 1 cut partridge + giblets
- 1 tsp (5 g) ground cinnamon
- 1 tsp (5 g) ginger powder
- 1 onion
- 1 handful fresh coriander
- 1 cup (200 ml) water
- 1 tbsp (10 g) pine nuts
- 1 tbsp (14 g) vinegar
- ¼ cup (50 g) olive oil
- ½ cup (100 g) water
- 10 mint leaves
- 10 lemon leaves (preserved if it if possible)
- chopped liver and gizzards
- 3 beaten eggs
- 6 half hard-boiled egg yolks
- 5 mint leaves
- ½ tbsp toasted pine nuts
- ½ tbsp pistachios
- ½ tbsp rose water

The fourth explicitly Jewish recipe of the Kitāb al-ṭabīẖ is called لون من حجلة يهودى*, which means “A* ***Jewish*** *dish of Partridge.” It is a simpler recipe than the previous partridge one.*

Pluck and cut the partridge into four parts.

Place the partridge in a large frying pan and add the spices such as cinnamon and ginger.

Prepare the juice of both onion and fresh green coriander, by mixing these two ingredients with water and crushing the resulting puree to release the juice.

Pour this juice into the frying pan, with the partridge and the other ingredients.

Add whole pine nuts, vinegar, oil, water, mint and lemon leaves, chopped liver and gizzards, and the 3 beaten eggs. Cover and cook for 30 minutes over medium heat.

To garnish, add 12 half hard-boiled egg yolks in a star shape around the partridge.

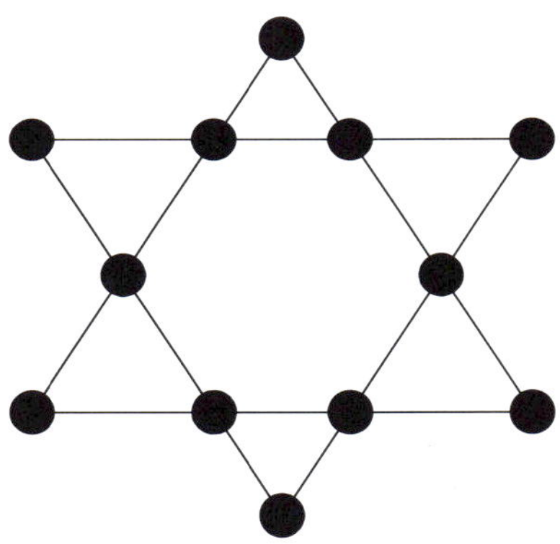

Also add mint leaves, toasted pine nuts, pistachios, and rose water.

Serve immediately.

"A stuffed buried Jewish dish"

Serves 8
Time: 2 hours

For the ground meat:

- 1 lb (450 g) ground meat
- ¼ cup (50 g) olive oil
- 1 tbsp ground ginger
- 1 tsp rose water
- 1 tsp salt
- 1 onion mixed

For the meatballs:

- 1 lb (450 g) ground meat
- ¼ cup (50 g) olive oil
- 1 tbsp ground ginger
- 1 tbsp cumin
- 1 onion, very finely chopped
- 2 garlic cloves, chopped
- 1 tsp salt

For the omelet layers:

- 5 eggs
- 1 tsp salt
- 1 tsp black pepper
- ½ tsp ground cinnamon
- ⅛ cup (25 g) olive oil

To decorate:

- 1 tbsp olive oil
- 3 eggs, beaten
- 1 tbsp flour
- 1 tsp black pepper
- 1 tsp ground cinnamon
- 1 tsp rose water
- mint leaves
- 1 tbsp crushed pistachios
- 1 tbsp toasted pine nuts

This is the fifth explicitly Jewish recipe of the Kitāb al-ṭabīẖ. It is called لون يهودى محشو مدفون, *meaning "A Stuffed Buried* ***Jewish*** *dish." This recipe combines several culinary techniques, such as omelets and meatballs, and the final result looks like a large layered cake. The instruction to use a new cooking pot, combined with all the other clues of Jewishness disseminated in this thirteenth-century Western Muslim recipe, finds an echo in the trials of the Portuguese Inquisition of the end of the sixteenth century: Cecilia and Felipa Cardosa, from the Portuguese city of Coimbra, were charged with preparing matza "in a new pot" to celebrate Passover. This recipe uses not one but three different pots.*

Start by placing the ground meat in a (new, if you want to follow the original recipe to the letter) frying pan. Use one with high sides. Add olive oil, ground ginger, rose water, water, and salt. Mix in the onion.

Stir all with a large spoon and cook over a medium heat for 5 minutes. Remove from the heat and set aside in a large bowl.

Now, for the meatballs/*albóndigas*: add ginger, cumin, very finely chopped onion, garlic, and salt to the ground meat.

Form small balls, all the same size.

Pour olive oil in the same pan used to cook the ground meat, and heat it over medium heat. Cook the meatballs, without turning them, for 2 minutes. Then turn them over and cook for another 2 minutes.

To prepare the two omelet layers, beat 5 eggs in a large bowl. Add salt, pepper, and ground cinnamon. Divide the mixture into two equal parts.

Add olive oil to a large frying pan (the omelets should be thin and wide in diameter). Heat slightly and pour in the first half of the egg mixture. Cook for 2 minutes and turn to cook the other side. Set aside and prepare the second omelet in the same way.

Now to assemble the dish: place one omelet in the same frying pan, with some oil. It must go up the edges of the pan.

Spread the ground meat on top of the omelet to form an even layer. Cover with the second omelet. This time it does not need to go up the edges of the pan.

Add the meatballs on top, to form another layer.

In a bowl, beat 3 eggs. Add flour, pepper, cinnamon, and rose water. Pour over the meatballs.

Cover the pan and cook for 30 minutes over low heat. Then, take the lid off and let stand for 15 minutes or more, so that it all thickens and comes together.

Prepare a large and completely flat serving plate. Turn it upside down onto the frying pan. Firmly, hold both the frying pan and the large dish, and turn over. The dish will look like a large cake.

Garnish with mint twigs, crushed pistachios, and toasted pine nuts.

“A Jewish dish of eggplants stuffed with meat”

Serves 4
Time: 1 hour 30 minutes

- 5 small or medium eggplants

For the ground meat:

- ½ pound (220 g) ground meat (beef or lamb)
- 1 tsp salt
- 1 tsp pepper
- ½ tsp cinnamon
- 2 egg whites
- 1 cup (120 g) breadcrumbs (optional)

In pot no. 1:

- 2 tbsp olive oil
- ¼ cup (45 g) mixed onions
- 2 cloves chopped garlic
- ½ tsp ground ginger
- ⅓ cup (20 g) chopped fresh green cilantro
- ½ tsp salt
- ½ tsp rose water
- 1 tbsp pine nuts
- 1 tbsp etrog leaves (or lemon)
- 1tbsp chopped mint leaves
- ¼ cup (50 g) water

In pot no. 2:

- 2 tbsp olive oil
- 1 tbsp vinegar
- 1 chopped onion
- 1 garlic clove, chopped
- ½ tsp ginger
- 3 sprigs of oregano
- 3 strands of rue
- ½ tbsp etrog leaves (or lemon)
- ¼ cup (30 g) fennel tips
- 1 tbsp almonds, chopped
- ⅓ cup (130 g) chickpeas, cooked
- 2 saffron strands
- ¼ cup (50 g) water
- 3 egg yolks, hard boiled

This dish is the last explicitly Jewish recipe of the Kitāb al-ṭabīḫ. *It is entitled* لون يهودى من باذنجان محشو بلحم, *meaning “A Jewish dish of Eggplants stuffed with meat.” For me, this is the recipe that brings together the largest number of features of the Sephardic Jews' diet: eggplants, stuffing, a long cooking time, and a particular aesthetic. This recipe is the longest of all, and it is also technically difficult. Eggs are used in different forms: whites for binding, hard-boiled yolks for decorating. The ingredients list is long and three different pots are used, so that certain ingredients are kept separate. Again, there are pine nuts added at the end, as well as rose water. The addition of acidic liquids at several different times during the preparation (and in large quantities) is noteworthy, as it points to a predilection for tangy flavors by Sephardic Jews: vinegar, including a “spicy” kind, and* murrī, *a sauce created by the long fermentation of bread in water, salt, and various spices.*

Cook the eggplants in salted boiling water for 20 minutes. Cut them in two equal parts lengthwise. Hollow them out, taking care not to damage the skin since it will be stuffed.

Prepare the ground meat: add it to a large bowl with the salt, pepper, cinnamon, and 2 egg whites. Add the flesh of the eggplants. Fill the eggplants with this stuffing. You can put breadcrumbs over the eggplant, it will be crunchier.

Prepare three pots:

In pot no. 1, add all ingredients and cook over low heat for 10 minutes.

In pot no. 2, add all ingredients minus the yolks, and place half of the stuffed eggplants on top. Cover and cook for 20 minutes. Decorate the pot with chopped egg yolks.

Do the same for pot no. 3, placing the other half of the stuffed eggplants on top. Garnish with black pepper and a fresh egg yolk.

Bring all three pots to the table. Serve from pots no. 2 and no. 3 first, and then pour over the sauce from pot no. 1.

In pot no. 3:

- 2 tbsp olive oil
- 1 tbsp chopped cilantro
- 1 tbsp vinegar
- 1 onion, chopped
- 1 tbsp crushed almonds
- 1 tbsp pine nuts
- 3 strands of rue
- ½ tbsp etrog leaves (or lemon)
- ½ tsp rose water
- ¼ tsp black pepper
- 1 fresh egg yolk

In April 1483, the Catholic monarchs installed an Inquisition tribunal in the Spanish city of Ciudad Real, south of Madrid. In 1511, Catalina de Teva, conversa, was denounced—by her servant—for her Jewish culinary practices, such as making casseroles of stuffed eggplants for Shabbat, which she and her friends ate cold on Saturdays. The recipe we just presented, from the thirteenth century, closely resembles the one prepared almost 300 years later by the conversos of Spain.

Makābīb la'nūhā al-yahūd
"Meatballs cursed by the Jews"

Makes 25
Time: 45 minutes

- 1 lb (450 g) beef ground meat
- ¼ tsp black pepper
- 1 tsp salt
- ⅓ cup (20 g) chopped parsley
- 10 chopped mint leaves
- 10 chopped celery leaves
- 1 egg, beaten
- 3/4 cup (150 g) neutral oil (for frying)

As we mentioned, among Eastern Muslim cookbooks of the Middle Ages, the only one to contain explicitly Jewish recipes is the Kitāb al-waṣf al-aṭ'ima al-mu'tāda *[The Description of Familiar Foods], where the following recipe is found. The title mentioning a "curse" is intriguing (مكابيب لعنو ها اليهود), since there is no indication of what it means in the cookbook. Why were these meatballs "cursed" by the Jews? We are left to draw our own conclusions...*

In the most recent copy of Kitāb al-waṣf al-aṭ'ima al-mu'tāda *(seventeenth/eighteenth century), the recipe above is replaced by a very similar one called "Meatballs of the Jews." No explanation is given on the replacement, and why the term "cursed" is no longer used.*

Boil some water, and cook the meat in it for just 10 seconds. Take it out.

Put the meat into a large bowl (having drained any water) and add the black pepper, salt, parsley, mint, and celery leaves. Mix together.

Beat the egg and pour it over the meat mixture.

Pour the oil into a frying pan and heat over medium heat.

With the meat mixture, form small balls the size of walnuts.

Fry them for 3 minutes without moving them. Then, turn them over and cook for another 3 minutes until golden, and serve.

המאור

MEAT AND FISH

"[For Shabbat] a pot of mutton or cow innards, and stewed hands and feet and hoofs, cooked from early Friday and all night until Saturday"

Trial from the Spanish Inquisition court of Cuenca, 1505

"[On Friday, Isabel Gonzales used to] to cook fish stews and sardines, sometimes with eggplants, onions, coriander and spices."

Trial against the *converso* Isabel Gonzales, from the Spanish Inquisition court of Ciudad Real, 1494

"the meat of sheep that are one or two years old, the meat of chicken, the francolin, the grouse, the turtle dove and the partridge [are good food]"

Maimonides,

***Regimen of Health*, Chapter I (1198)**

Adefina
The iconic slow-cooked chickpea and beef stew

Serves 4-6
Time: 1 hour + overnight

- ½ lb (220 g) beef brisket, bone in, or lamb neck
- 2 tbsp sugar
- water (to cover the meat)
- 1 onion
- ⅓ cup (66 g) olive oil
- 2 bay leaves
- 1 tbsp salt
- 1 whole head garlic
- ½ tsp ground cinnamon
- ½ tsp black pepper
- ½ tsp ground nutmeg
- ½ tsp turmeric
- 1 cup (200 g) chickpeas (soaked in water 24 hours before)
- 6 hard-boiled eggs in their shell
- 10 dates
- 1 cup (175 g) Swiss chard, boiled
- 10 mint leaves
- water

For the fried rice:

- 2 tbsp olive oil
- ½ cup (100 g) rice
- 1 clove garlic, chopped
- ½ tsp salt
- ½ tsp turmeric
- 2 saffron strands
- a muslin

Adefina, adafina, dafina, aní, hamín, caliente, trasnochado. *All these names refer to one thing: the quintessential Shabbat dish of the Sephardic Jews of the fifteenth century. It was commonly known under different names, and this would have been one way Jews were able to deceive Inquisition officials, as this dish would have revealed the makers and eaters as Jewish. All terms refer to the characteristics of the dish:* adefina, adafina, dafina *mean "buried, hidden."* Aní, hamín, caliente *refer to the fact that the dish is "hot." And* trasnochado *refers to the fact that it is cooked "overnight."*

Out of respect for the history of this recipe, the method presented here does not contain the "New World" ingredients—like potatoes and sweet potatoes—that are frequently used nowadays by Sephardim to prepare adefina.

Add the meat (bone in) to a large ovenproof pot with the sugar. Brown for 5 minutes over high heat. Add water just to cover the meat and boil for 10 minutes. With a skimmer, remove and discard the layer of fat that forms over the water.

In the same water, add the onion (whole), olive oil, bay leaves, salt, one whole head of garlic, ground cinnamon, black pepper, ground nutmeg, and turmeric without overlapping if possible.

Add the chickpeas, the hard-boiled eggs, dates, chard, mint leaves.

Meanwhile, make the fried rice separately: take a frying pan and add the olive oil, rice, garlic, salt, turmeric, and saffron. Brown for 5 minutes over low medium heat. Let it cool, put everything in muslin and tie it.

Add the muslin to the pot with the meat.

Add water to cover all ingredients. Cover the pot and place it in the oven at the end of the afternoon, at 200°F (100 °C). It will be ready the next day at the end of the morning.

You can serve the different ingredients from the pot (rice, eggs, vegetables, broth, meat) in separate dishes.

Many conversos *were denounced to the Inquisition by their own servants, who became suspicious when they were forbidden from preparing food for Friday evening, and sent out of the house when it was time to prepare the* adefina *or the* hamín. *There were many versions of this dish documented in Inquisition trial records throughout the fifteenth century. All have some variation in the ingredients, but they often contain meat and olive oil, and are cooked overnight for Shabbat.*

Andrés Bernáldez (1415–1513) mentioned the term "adafina" in relation to the culinary practices of the Jews. In the Memoirs of the Reign of the Catholic Monarchs (*fifteenth century*), *he wrote that* adafina *was "a pot-au-feu* (puchero) *or pot* (olla) *that the Jews place at nightfall on a stove covering it with embers, for eating on Saturdays." Various Spanish literary works testify to the preparation and consumption of* adefina *between the fourteenth and sixteenth centuries, including the* Libro de Buen amor, *the* Cancionero de Baena, *the* Copla a Pedro González, *and the* Cancionero general.

Cecina and *namkasūd* Dried meat

Serves 8-10
Time: 3 weeks or more

- 2 pounds (900 g) brisket beef
- ½ cup vinegar
- 8 cups (1.6 l) water
- 4 cups (1 kg) coarse salt
- 2 tbsp black pepper
- 2 tbsp coriander seeds
- 2 tbsp cumin seeds
- 2 tbsp caraway seeds

A dish of dried beef meat, now commonly known as cecina, *is mentioned in the thirteenth-century cookbook from Al Andalus* Fuḍālat al-ẖiwān. *Its author, Ibn Razīn al-Tuǧībī, tells us that his recipe resembles one written by Yonah Ibn Ǧanāḥ (tenth-eleventh century), a Cordovan grammarian and physician of Jewish origin, who in his work* Kitāb tafsīr al-adwiya *[Treatise on the explanation of drugs] presents a recipe of salted and dried meat called* namkasūd. *Ibn explains that the main difference between the two is that "the* namkasūd *is made with a whole ram or cut into two halves; the meat remains tender and fatty, when you press it down your hand digs in and the knife cuts it as if it were fresh meat, not like cutting dried meat." Here both versions are presented, for you to choose which you prefer.*

For *cecina*:

In a saucepan, boil the vinegar and water. Add the salt and half of the spices. Cook until the salt is completely dissolved. Set aside until the water is cold.

Then put the beef in the vinegary solution. The meat must be completely covered. Put it in the fridge for a week or two. The meat must never come out of the water.

Remove the meat, rinse it with clean water, put it in a large bowl of clean water for at least 4 hours.

Dry the meat with a paper towel and coat it with the rest of the crushed spices.

You can leave it to dry in a ventilated place—wrapped in cheesecloth—for at least a week; or put it under the grill at the lowest setting for two hours, or even on barbeque embers to smoke for two hours, and then let it out to dry. Cut it into thin slices. You can keep it in an airtight box in the refrigerator for weeks.

For *namkasūd*:

Put the coarse salt in a dish just the size of the piece of meat. Place the meat on top and cover it completely with salt. Leave to cool for 72 hours.

Take the meat out of the salt and put it in a bowl of clear water for 4 hours, changing the water every hour. Take the meat out of the water and dry it. Cover it with the ground spices, pressing well all over so that they stick to the meat. Wrap it in a clean cloth and tie the bundle well with string. Then, put the meat in the bottom of the refrigerator for a month. Finally, take it out, remove the excess spices and cut it into thin slices. You can keep it in an airtight box in the refrigerator for weeks.

The first record of a recipe for dried meat, called ṣfa qadīd, *is found in another* Kitāb al-ṭabīẖ, *this time from the tenth century and written by Ibn Sayyār al-Warrāq. The recipe is particularly interesting because it states that this dish, accompanied by flat bread and fermented sauce or tahini sauce, can be offered "for those who drink wine." Reference is made here to non-Muslims and therefore most likely to Jews, given the similarities that existed in their diet; although one cannot rule out the possibility that this also applies to Eastern Christians the first theory seems to be more probable, because the reference to thin, flat bread can possibly indicate* matza, *or unleavened bread, which is eaten by Jews on Passover.*

The preparation of this dish did not escape the eye of the Inquisition. Don Gonçalo, a jeweler from the northern Spanish city of Soria, was convicted in the late fifteenth century because his family prepared "dried beef [çeçina de vaca] [...], and to prepare it as the Jews do, the wife and daughters of Gonçalo the jeweler were porging [...] the meat."

The Sephardim were known for their expertise in preparing cecina, *and this is highlighted in many Inquisition records. Ultimately, the Inquisition courts forbade the making of dried meat because of its Jewish associations, despite the fact that Spanish Christians also ate and described it in their cookbooks of the sixteenth and seventeenth centuries.*

Tharīd
Thick soup with unleavened bread and chicken

Serves 6
Time: 2 hours

- 1 chicken
- 2 tsp salt
- 1 large onion
- ½ tsp black pepper
- ½ tsp ground coriander
- 3 tbsp olive oil
- ⅛ cup (23 g) fenugreek seeds

For the bowl:

- ⅓ cup (66 g) olive oil
- 3 tbsp water

For the *faṭīr* dough:

- 2 cup (300 g) flour
- 2 cup (300 g) extra fine semolina
- 1 tsp salt
- 2 cups (400 ml) lukewarm water

To decorate:

- 6 eggs yolks
- 10 green olives
- ¼ tsp ground cinnamon
- 1 tbsp whole almonds

Tharīd *is a dish that existed in territories under Muslim domination since the Middle Ages, and was eaten by Andalusians of all religions. It is mentioned in the* Kitāb al-ṭabīẖ*, and the recipe below is adapted from that very version, referred to as the "*Tharīd *called* faṭīr *[unleavened bread] by the people of Ifriquya [Tunisia]." The instructions are often symbolic, such as arranging the egg yolks "like stars." This dish is similar to the* rfissa *or* trid *still consumed in Morocco nowadays, and it is in fact also mentioned in another source concerning fifteenth-century Fez, known as a place where Jews have always lived.*

Cut the chicken into pieces, keeping the skin on.

Take a pot and add salt, an onion cut into 6, black pepper, dry coriander, and oil. Cook for 2 minutes over high heat. Then, add the cut chicken and pour water until the halfway mark on the pot. Cover and cook over low heat for 30 minutes with the lid on.

Meanwhile, prepare the unleavened *faṭīr* bread. In a large bowl, add the flour, salt and lukewarm water. Mix with a large spoon, then once the dough forms into a ball, knead with your hands for 15 minutes. The dough should be smooth. Cover it and put it in the fridge for 15 minutes.

Prepare a bowl with olive oil and water, and sprinkle some on the kitchen counter.

Take a chunk of dough the size of a golf ball. Spread it with your fingers on the greased kitchen counter. Roll it out as thin as you can without letting it rip, keeping a disk shape. Be careful, it is very fragile.

Then, fold it: the upper part to the middle, then the lower part to the upper part. You will get a strip of dough. Now, take the right end and fold it to the middle, then take the left end and fold it over. You will get a square (with several folds). Do the same with the rest of the dough.

Heat a large greased pan. When all the squares are ready, take the first one. Use your fingers to spread it out, keeping the square shape and without breaking it, until it is three times the width of a hand. Put in the hot pan and cook for 2 minutes on each side. Once the puff pastry square is cooked, break it up into small pieces. Place these crumbs on a large serving dish.

Uncover the pot with the chicken. Take all the chicken pieces and grill them at medium heat in the oven for 10 minutes. Meanwhile, cook the sauce over high heat for 5 minutes.

Then, place the chicken pieces on the *faṭīr* breadcrumbs in the large dish. Drizzle the chicken and crumbs with all the sauce from the pot.

Decorate with hard-boiled egg yolks (arranging them like stars), olives, whole almonds (preferably toasted), and sprinkle with cinnamon.

Many Jews lived in Morocco in the fifteenth century. Ibn al-Ahmar wrote that "Among the mawālī *[non-Arabs who converted to Islam in conquered territories, including Jews], there were those who worked in the baking of bread,* sfenğ, *and pastries. They roasted meat, they made cooking pots and sold them. They squeezed the oil from olives and transported it, along with soap, to sell it. They sold salt, fish and fat. They made* fānīd. *They sold medicines and medicinal plants. They were servants in public baths, carried water, carved wood, cooked* fidāwīsh, sha'riyya, tharīd, maqrūt *and* raghaīf *to sell them."*

Oriza
Wheat grain and chicken stew

Serves 4–6
Time: 30 minutes + all night

- 2 cup (300 g) wheat grain (whole if possible)
- ½ cup (100 g) olive oil
- 2 onions, sliced
- 3 garlic cloves, crushed
- 2 tbsp sugar
- ½ lb (or less, 220 g) chicken breasts
- 1 tsp salt
- ½ tsp black pepper
- 3 strands of saffron (or ¼ tsp food coloring)
- 4 hard-boiled eggs, peeled (optional)
- 2 potatoes and 2 sweet potatoes (optional, as they were unknown to thirteenth-century Europe)

The dish named harīsa *was one of the most popular dishes in al-Andalus. It could be made at home or bought at the souk. The name comes from the Arabic "harīs" (هريس) meaning "ground," "pounded." The* Kitāb al-ṭabīẖ *cookbook includes harīsa recipes, and it states that they should be made with ⅔ wheat and ⅓ meat. The meat used can be breast or thighs of chicken or goose, but also lamb or veal. The dish is cooked in the oven, overnight, similarly to dishes made for Shabbat. Nowadays, a very similar dish is still prepared by Sephardic Jews, mainly from Morocco. The name has hardly changed: it is called* oriza *(or* adafina de trigo*, i.e. wheat* adafina*).*

Leave the wheat in water for a whole day. The next day, drain it and rub it dry.

In an oven-safe pot, pour the olive oil, the onion, garlic, and sugar. Add the wheat and brown for 5 minutes.

Add the chicken breasts, sprinkling with salt, black pepper, and saffron. Mix and pour in 1 cup of water. Cook for 5 minutes, stirring.

Cover completely with water (about 3 cups) and add the hard-boiled eggs, as well as the potatoes and sweet potatoes, cut into large pieces (if using).

At the end of the day, cover this pot with a lid, and put it in the oven at 150°F (70°C) until noon the next day.

Meat pie of the Fernandes *conversos* from Bahia

Serves 6
Time: 1 hour

For the dough:

- 2 eggs
- 1 ¾ cup (280 g) flour
- ½ tsp salt
- ⅓ cup (75 g) soft butter or margarine
- egg wash

For the filling:

- ¼ cup (50 g) olive oil
- 2 cloves of garlic, chopped
- 2 onions, sliced
- ½ pound (220 g) ground meat
- 3 eggs, beaten
- ¼ cup (15 g) fresh coriander
- 2 tsp ground cumin
- 1 tsp salt
- 1 tsp black pepper
- egg wash
- 1 tbsp oregano
- 1 tbsp sesame seeds

Pies were a favorite dish of conversos. *This recipe is based on a 1590 Inquisition trial record, which explains how the Fernandes family from Bahia, Brazil, were reported for their Shabbat cooking: preparing a baked dish of meat with onion, olive oil, seeds, spices and other ingredients, sealed with dough all around. The excellent cookbook* A Drizzle of Honey *also offers a recipe for this dish.*

To make the dough, beat the eggs, and add the flour and salt. Add the soft margarine (or oil). Mix all the ingredients together. Knead the dough for 5 minutes until even and smooth. Split the dough in 2 balls, cover, and put in the fridge for 30 minutes.

For the filling, pour the olive oil into a frying pan, add the garlic and onions. Fry for 3 minutes until golden.

Add the ground meat and cook for 5 minutes at medium-high heat. Then place the mixture in a big bowl to cool.

In another bowl, beat the 3 eggs. Add the salt, black pepper, fresh coriander, and cumin, and mix.

Then, add the cooked ground meat (drained of its liquid) to the mixture.

Turn on the oven at 375°F (190°C).

Roll out the first ball of dough between two pieces of parchment paper, until it is a tenth of an inch thick (a couple of millimeters). Do the same with the second ball. Lay the first disk of dough in a pie dish.

Add the filling, without reaching the top. Cover with the second disk of dough, flattening the edges. Refrigerate for at least 30 minutes.

Brush the pie with egg wash and sprinkle with oregano and sesame seeds. Prick the dough in the middle with the tip of a knife. Bake for 40 minutes.

Let it cool for 15 minutes before serving.

Converso fish stew

Serves 4
Time: 40 minutes

- ½ cup (100 g) olive oil
- 2 garlic cloves, chopped
- 1 onion, sliced thinly
- ¼ lb (110 g) salted fish (e.g., cod)
- ½ lb (220 g) fresh white fish (e.g., cod or hake)
- ¼ lb (110 g) fresh tuna
- ½ tsp salt
- ½ cup (100 g) water
- ⅛ cup (30 g) vinegar
- ½ cup (60 g) chopped chives
- 3 eggs
- 2 cups (400 g) cooked chickpeas
- 1 lime

In the Iberian Peninsula of the Middle Ages, just like today, it was very common to eat fish on Shabbat; this did not escape the Inquisitors. On January 20, 1486, in the Spanish town of Aranda, Juan Sanches and his family were denounced for eating barbs and fish for their Saturday night dinner. The conger eel is also a type of fish mentioned in these trials. Fried eggs and sardines were eaten by the Sephardim during the Christian Lent period, whose end coincides roughly with Passover.

This fish stew for Shabbat is a dish which crossed the Atlantic, as one particular Inquisition trial from Mexico reveals: Ruy Díaz Nieto, a practicing Sephardic Jew originally from Porto, Portugal, mentions that on Shabbat he ate a fish stew made with chickpeas, eggs, salted fish, fresh fish and tuna—just like the one below.

In a pot, pour the olive oil and add the chopped garlic, onion, and salt. Cook for 3 minutes over medium heat. Add the drained chickpeas and cook for 5 minutes.

Wash the fish and cut it into cubes. Add the pieces to the pot together with the tuna and the salted fish, and pour in the vinegar and the water. Then, sprinkle half of the finely cut chives. Cover and cook for 15 minutes over low heat, without stirring.

Break the eggs into the pot, around the fish chunks, and cook the stew on a low heat, covered, for 5 minutes.

Uncover, sprinkle with the juice of half the lime and the rest of the cut chives, and serve with the other half lime.

Converso fish pie

Makes 7 small pies
Time: 1 hour

For the dough:

- 2 eggs
- 1 ¾ cup (280 g) flour
- ½ tsp salt
- ⅓ cup (75 g) soft butter or margarine
- Egg wash

For the filling:

- ¼ cup (50 g) olive oil
- 1 garlic clove, chopped
- 1 onion
- 1 lb (400 g) fresh white fish (cod or hake)
- 1 cup (100 g to 150 g) grated cheese
- 3 eggs, beaten
- ½ tsp salt
- 1 tsp black pepper

The recipe for this fish pie was not mentioned in the records, but it is regarded as one of the many ways conversos *were identified and denounced. It was very much part of the culinary practices of the* converso *Jews of Mexico and Brazil, and was generally eaten during the feast of Yom Kippur, to break the fast.*

To make the dough, beat the eggs, and add flour and salt. Add the soft margarine (or oil). Mix all the ingredients together. Knead the dough for 5 minutes until even and smooth. Cover and put in the fridge for 30 minutes.

Meanwhile, prepare the filling: add the olive oil, garlic, and chopped onion to a pan. Fry for 3 minutes until golden.

Add the fish and sauté for 5 minutes at medium heat. Transfer to a big bowl to cool.

In another bowl, mix the grated cheese and 2 eggs. Add salt and black pepper. Then, add the fish mixture.

Roll out the dough between two pieces of parchment paper until it is a tenth of an inch thick (a couple of millimeters). To prepare the first individual pie, cut out a circle with a round cookie cutter (2 in/5cm diameter, or in any case larger than your pie dish). Grease the pie dish, lay the first disk of dough in it and raise it around the edges to the top.

Add in the filling, leaving some room at the top. Cut out another dough circle and cover the top of the pie. Flatten the edges. Do the same for the rest of your small pies. Once finished, refrigerate for at least 30 minutes.

Turn on the oven to 400°F (200°C). Take your cold fish pies out of the fridge and put them on a tray. Brush them with egg wash, and prick the top with a knife. Once the oven is hot, cook them for 25 minutes.

Wait until the pies have cooled to remove them from their molds.

PARACHAT A'HAREI MOT

ספר ויקרא
פרשת אחרי מות
PARACHAT A'HAREI MOT

LEWIS STAGNETTO
ESTABLISHED 1870
TOBACCONIST
WINES AND SPIRITS
41
VISA
Boux
SONIC

TWO YOM KIPPUR MENUS OF *CONVERSOS* FROM MEXICO

Along with the celebration of Shabbat, the feast of Yom Kippur ("Quipur," or "El día Grande") is the one most mentioned in Inquisition sources, as an opportunity to identify *conversos* through their cooking, and above all, their fasting. Here is a selection of the food two Mexican *conversos* ate for Yom Kippur in the mid-seventeenth century.

Gaspar Váez
1640

Serves 4
Time: 30 minutes

- 4 *huebos hammados* or hard-boiled eggs (see p. 36)
- 1 green salad leaves of your choosing
- 4 small fish pies (see p. 84)
- 4 slices of smoked tuna, or 4 sardines in oil, or 8 anchovies marinated in oil
- 1 cup black and green olives
- hot chocolate

In Mexico, to break the fast, Gaspar Váez had a dinner of eggs, salad, empanadas, fish, olives and hot chocolate. No meat. Because it was seen as a festive drink, chocolate could substitute the wine used for the Kiddush of Shabbat. When added to the fasting and secretive behavior, drinking chocolate was another telltale sign of converso *customs.* A Drizzle of Honey *also offers a recipe for this dish.*

Prepare *huebos hammados* or hard-boiled eggs. Cut them in half.

Prepare the fish pies.

Chop or tear the salad leaves.

In a dish, arrange sardines, or smoked fish, or anchovies.

Place green and black olives in a small bowl.

Prepare a glass of hot chocolate your favorite way, and enjoy.

Salomón Machorro 1650

Serves 4
Time: 30 minutes

- 4 *huebos hammados* (see p. 36)
- bread (such as matza, see p. 24)
- 1 ½ cup (220 g) cheese (mature or fresh)
- wine

Salomón Machorro, from Mexico City, is also known as Juan de León Pacheco. The trials of the inquisition tell us that he ate roasted eggs, bread, cheese and wine, after the ritual bath, before Yom Kippur started. A recipe for this is also found in A Drizzle of Honey.

Prepare the *huebos hammados*. Cut them in half.

Bake the bread, and cut it into slices. Serve it hot.

In a dish, arrange slices of mature cheese.

Pour some wine and enjoy.

SOUPS

"One should take a little of what is customary, and always maintain his strength by taking nourishment, either light nourishment like chicken soup, meat broth, yolk or soft-boiled eggs."

Maimonides,
Regimen of Health, Chapter II (1198)

Fidāwīsh
Short vermicelli noodles with tuna, saffron, and mint

Serves 4-5
Time: 30 minutes

- ½ cup (100 g) olive oil
- 5 garlic cloves, chopped
- 3 tomatoes
- 1 onion, sliced
- 3 green peppers, sliced
- 3 tsp salt
- 3 cup (400 g) short vermicelli noodles
- 2 saffron strands (or ⅛ tsp food coloring)
- ½ cup (280 g) tuna (fresh or canned)
- 1 handful of mint, chopped
- 6 cups (1.5 l) water

Fidāwīsh *was prepared and consumed, probably in markets, by Moroccan Jews in the fifteenth century. Even if we can attest to this culinary practice only in the imperial city of Fez, we can guess it was present in the rest of the territory as well.* Fidāwīsh *also appears in the first and only cookbook of the West Middle Ages that contains Jewish recipes, the* Kitab al-ṭabīẖ *(thirteenth century). Here is a reconstruction of the dish, albeit including food unknown to the area at the time such as green peppers and tomatoes.*

In a pan, pour the olive oil, garlic, chopped tomatoes, onion, green peppers, and salt. Fry for 5 minutes.

Add the vermicelli noodles (*fideos* in Spanish) and the saffron, mix well, and cook slowly for 2 minutes. Boil the water and then pour it in the pan. Add the chopped mint and tuna. Mix carefully.

Cook it slowly for 15 minutes, and serve hot.

Puchero
Maimonides' chicken soup

Serves 4
Time: 30 minutes

- ½ pound (220 g) chicken breast
- 2 or 3 tbsp olive oil
- 1 clove garlic, chopped
- 3 carrots
- 2 stalks of celery, with leaves
- ½ cup (100 g) cooked chickpeas
- 1 onion
- 1 tsp salt
- ½ tsp black pepper
- 5 cups (1.5 l) water
- ½ cup (100 g) rice
- 4 eggs
- fresh lemon juice

In his book Regimen of Health *(1198), Maimonides writes that "The patient will always keep his strength by taking a light food like chicken soup, meat broth, soft egg yolk, wine for him who can take it, and even some less mild elements such as chicken meat." Maimonides' chicken soup reminds me of the one that my Andalusian grandmother used to make—also a dish that was mentioned in the Spanish Inquisition trial records of the sixteenth century. This dish nowadays bears the name* puchero.

Soften the chicken breasts by beating them, and cut them into small strips.

In a pot, heat the olive oil over medium heat. Add the chopped garlic clove and the pieces of chicken breast. Brown for 5 minutes.

Peel and wash the carrots. Cut them in half lengthwise, then cut them into pieces that are the width of two fingers. Put them in the pot.

Peel and wash the celery stalks. Cut them into finger-wide pieces and put them in the pot together with their leaves.

Add the cooked chickpeas, the onion cut into quarters, salt, pepper, and water. Cook covered for 15 minutes.

Then, add the rice and cook uncovered for 10 minutes. Add a little water if the mixture thickens.

In a separate saucepan, take 2 cups of the broth and bring to the boil. Crack an egg in the saucepan and move it around the pan so that the broth cooks it for 2 minutes, until soft boiled. Then place it in a bowl. Do the same for the other 3 eggs.

Pour the contents of the *puchero* in each bowl around the egg.

You can add a little fresh lemon juice for serving.

MAIMONIDES' *REGIMEN OF HEALTH* MENU

The *Regimen of Health* (1198) is a famous medical treaty written by the Andalusian doctor and rabbi Maimonides. It gives numerous indications on the ingredients and dishes which must be consumed to keep good health, asserting that food is the best medicine, just as Greek physician Galen had maintained many centuries prior. The *Regimen of Health* was written for Prince Al-Afdal, to help with his physical and mental health, as he suffered from indigestion, constipation, and depression.

Maimonides organized his patient's meal in courses. Firstly, a starter of green vegetables; then, a first course of broth (to soften the belly); the second course is left completely to the patient's choosing, and for Maimonides, as for many doctors of the antiquity, eating some of what one desires is part of the right cure; finally, a fruit dessert, as a diuretic.

Green vegetables sauté

Serves 2-4
Time: 30 minutes

- 1 small bunch of chard
- 1 cup (60 g) sorrel
- 1 ¼ pound (600 g) fresh spinach
- 1 cup (60 g) amaranth
- 1 tbsp olive oil
- ½ tsp salt

Here is the recipe for the starter: "seasoned vegetables (chard, sorrel, spinach, amaranth)."

Wash the vegetables.

Pour the olive oil into a pan.

Add all the leaves and sauté them over medium high heat for 10 minutes.

Add the salt and olive oil before serving.

Gazpachuelo
Lemon broth

Serves 4
Time: 30 minutes

- 4 cups (1 l) water with 1 tsp salt dissolved
- 1 egg white
- 1 egg yolk
- ⅛ cup (25 g) olive oil
- 1 saffron strand (or ⅛ tsp food coloring)
- 1 tsp sugar (optional)
- the juice of a fresh lemon + 1 lemon slice per plate
- bread croutons

The first course is lemon broth. This dish is still prepared in Andalusia and bears the name of "gazpachuelo."

Heat up the salted water, and once it boils, pour in the egg white. Drain and set aside, keeping the hot water.

Make a mayonnaise-type sauce: beat the egg yolk in a large bowl with a whisk or a fork. Gradually add olive oil. Beat for 10–15 minutes until you get a firm consistency. In another bowl, take 1 tablespoon of the hot salted water used to cook the egg white and add 2 tablespoons of cold water. While mixing the mayonnaise, pour the water in very slowly. Add saffron and sugar (optional).

Very gradually, add the rest of the hot salted water to the mayonnaise. Be careful: if you pour too quickly, the egg yolk will coagulate.

Pour the *gazpachuelo* and the pieces of cooked egg white into four bowls. Add fresh lemon juice and a lemon slice.

Serve hot with croutons.

Quince, Pear, Apple, and Pomegranate Juice

Serves 2–4
Time: 30 minutes

- 2 pears
- 2 apples
- 2 cups (0.5 l) water
- 2 tbsp honey
- 2 tbsp quince jelly
- 3 tsp pomegranate syrup (optional)
- 1 pomegranate (seeds)

A diuretic juice, great for cleansing the body.

Wash the pears and apples. Cut them into very small pieces.

Pour the water into a saucepan and add 2 tbsp of honey. Add the fruit and the quince jelly. Cover and cook for 15 minutes.

Cool and filter, so only the liquid is left. If desired, mix in the fruit.

Pour the juice into a bottle and refrigerate.

Just before serving, shake the bottle very well. You can now add the pomegranate syrup.

Decorate with pomegranate seeds.

DESSERTS AND PASTRIES

“They made huts with branches [for Sukkot] [...] where they did all the ceremonies that Jews used to do in those days, eating inside those and making collations with candy nougat and other things”

Trial against Juan Sánchez Exarch,
a Spanish *converso* from Teruel, 1484

“Many times [the accuser] saw that he ate meat on Fridays [for Shabbat] and cakes and pots of meat and *hamín* that Abrahén Romí gave him”

Trial against Juan López de Arnedo,
a Spanish *converso* from Soria, 1502

Murakkaba
The Moroccan *mufleta*

Serves 4
Time: 40 minutes

For the dough:

- 2 ¾ cup (430 g) flour
- 1 cup (150 g) extra-fine semolina
- ½ tbsp fresh yeast, crushed (or ½ tbsp active dry yeast, or 1 tbsp sourdough starter)
- ⅓ cup (66 ml) water (to mix with the yeast)
- 1 tsp salt
- 1 egg
- ⅛ cup (13 g) sugar
- 1 cup (200 ml) water
- neutral oil for frying
- sugar to sprinkle

For the drizzle:

- 1 cup (340 g) honey
- ½ cup (100 g) melted butter
- 10 dates chopped into small pieces

In the Kitāb al-ṭabīḫ *of Spain there are two recipes that correspond to the famous* mufleta, *which is still prepared today in the same way by Moroccan Sephardic Jews: "*Murakkaba*" and "*Murakkaba *Layered with Dates." This sweet dish is "composed" (*murakkaba *in Arabic) of alternating layers of dough "glued" to each other and turned upside down, a technique found throughout Jewish cuisine. Recipe titles may have varied throughout the ages, and ingredients may have been modified, but culinary techniques have remained intact.*

Mix the flour, the salt, the semolina, the yeast, and the lukewarm water in a pot. Knead for 10 minutes.

Form 8 small balls, brush them with oil and set aside for 15 minutes

Take one ball and flatten it out to form a very thin disc. Put it in a hot greasy pan for about 10 seconds, then turn it over. Flatten a second ball and put this new disc over the first one. Turn the two layers upside down. Flatten a third ball and place it on top, and keep going until you have no more disks left, turning upside down each time you form a new layer.

Chop the dates into small pieces and sprinkle them over the dish.

Place the tower on a serving plate. Pour melted butter and drizzle the honey over it.

Muhallabiyye
Almond rice pudding

Serves 6
Time: 30 minutes

- 1 cup (150 g) rice flour + 3/4 cup (170 ml) whole milk
- 2 cups (500 ml) almond milk
- 2 cups (500 ml) whole milk
- ½ cup (120 g) sugar
- 2 tsp orange blossom water
- 2 tbsp pomegranate syrup

*This is a version of a recipe prepared today in the Middle East by both Jewish and Muslim people. It has many different names and variations (*sutlage, mḥalbiya, malabi, ksab, mhallabiyye*), but what they all have in common is the use of rice or rice flour as a base. The dish is found in many cookbooks since the tenth century, often with the addition of sugar, saffron, and even chicken.*

Prepare the small jars or cups in which the preparation will be served.

In a bowl, mix the rice flour and milk with a fork.

In a saucepan, pour the almond milk and whole milk. Add the sugar and bring to a boil.

When it is boiling, lower the heat and add the rice flour and milk mixture.

Stir constantly for 3 minutes, to obtain a smooth consistency. It will thicken.

Add the orange blossom water.

Pour into the serving containers and let stand for 15 minutes.

Then, pour a dash of pomegranate syrup over it. Serve cold or at room temperature.

Nuegados
Orange and honey fried dough

Serves 4–6
Time: 40 minutes

- 3 tsp (13 g) olive oil
- peel of ½ lemon and orange
- 2 cup (300 g) flour
- ¼ cup (36 g) ground almonds
- ¼ cup (36 g) ground walnuts
- 3 eggs
- 1 tsp white wine (optional)
- 1 tsp sugar
- ¼ tsp baking powder
- neutral oil for frying

To drizzle:

- 1 cup (340 g) of honey
- 1 tsp orange blossom water (optional)

This dessert is part of the culinary heritage of Spain, particularly of the Northwest. What very few people know is that consuming this delicious dish led to the death of Spanish Jews and conversos*, such as Diego Arias from Medina de Campo (1490), who was reported for gifting* nuegados *and other fried pastries. Often made with breadcrumbs instead of flour, the dish is also mentioned in the book* La Lozana Andaluza *by Spanish* converso *Francisco Delicado: in the story, the Andalusian* conversa *Aldonza arrives in Rome after fleeing the Spanish Inquisition and tells women how she learned to prepare* nuegados *from her grandmother. Today, there is a fried pastry from the Campania Italian region called* struffoli. *It looks exactly like the Spanish* nuegados.

With a knife, peel the whole lemon and orange (without taking the pith). Add the peel to a frying pan with the olive oil. Fry over low heat, without burning the peel, for 3 minutes. Let cool.

Chop the orange and lemon peel. Keep the flavored oil.

Put the flour, ground almonds and walnuts into a large bowl, and make a hole in the center. Add the eggs, white wine (if using), sugar, and the flavored oil that you fried the zest in. Mix with a spoon starting from the center outward. Add the baking powder.

Put in a stand mixer with the hook attachment for 5 minutes, or knead by hand for 10 minutes. You can add more flour if the dough is too sticky, but it must remain elastic, so do not add too much.

With this dough, form long thin sausages, roughly the thickness of a finger. Shape all the dough in this way. It will dry out a bit and will be easier to handle.

Cut each strand into smaller chunks, roughly the width of a fingernail, with a sharp knife or a pair of scissors.

Heat up neutral oil in a frying pan or in a fryer at medium temperature.

Fry all pieces until they are golden. Be careful, they cook very quickly! Take them out of the oil and put them on a paper towel.

Heat the honey and orange blossom water in a saucepan. Do not let it boil.

Prepare a large plate in which to put the *nuegados*. You can also arrange them in portions using small cupcake or muffin liners.

In batches, stir the small fried pieces in the hot honey for 1 minute, and take them out with the skimmer.

Put the fried pieces on the plate or in the paper liners and let cool.

Isfenğ
The Andalusian donut

Makes 8
Time: 20 min + 4 hours (or overnight) + 20 min

- 1 tbsp fresh yeast + ⅓ cup (70 ml) lukewarm water
- 3 cups (450 g) flour
- 2 tsp sugar
- ½ tbsp salt
- 1 ⅔ cup (330 ml) lukewarm water
- neutral oil for frying

Also called sfenğ, *this fried pastry is common among Jews and Muslims especially in Morocco and Israel. It is also called* esponja *("sponge") in Spanish, a word derived from the Arabic term* sjenğ *of the same meaning. The recipe dates back to the thirteenth century, when this and similar dishes were popular in al-Andalus. Nowadays in Morocco, it is prepared by street vendors, although Jews mainly serve the dish for Hanukkah. This Jewish holiday is also known as "Festival of lights," and lasts for eight nights and eight days, to commemorate the miracle of the menorah candle in the Second Temple (168 BCE): the candle only had just enough oil to burn for a single day, but it lit the temple for eight nights leaving the Jews enough time to finish the temple's construction. It is in memory of this sacred oil that it is tradition to eat fried food for Hanukkah.*

In a small bowl, dilute the fresh yeast with lukewarm water.

In a large bowl, or in the bowl of a food processor, put the dissolved yeast, flour, sugar, and salt. Mix with the hook and gradually add the water. The dough should be sticky.

Mix for 15 minutes and cover the bowl. Rest overnight (or for at least 4 hours).

Then, heat the oil in a frying pan or in a deep fryer, over medium-high heat.

Lightly dip your hands into the water and take a portion of the dough (the size of a golf ball).

Make a hole in the middle of the dough and stretch it well. Then, fry the dough for 30 seconds to one minute, turning it over once.

These are usually eaten on their own, but you can sprinkle them with sugar and lightly dip them in honey if you want them to be sweet.

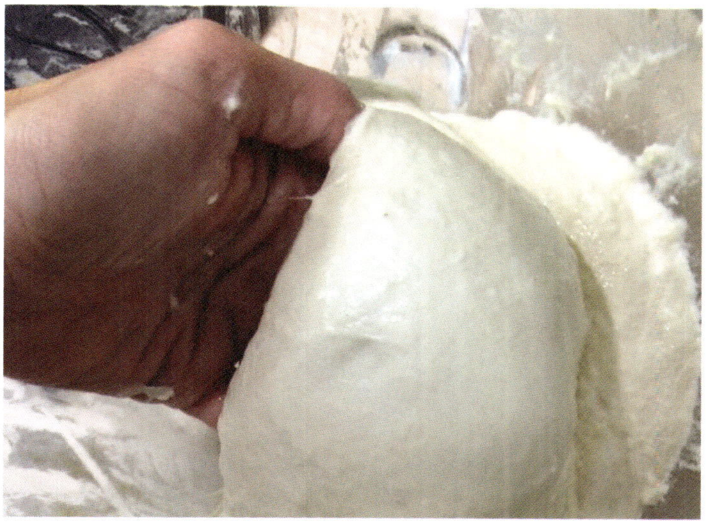

Maqrūṭ
Fried diamonds with dates and walnuts

Makes 40
Time: 2 hours 30 minutes

- 2 ½ cups (400 g) medium semolina
- ½ tsp salt
- ⅓ cup (80 g) melted butter
- 5 oz (150 g) dates (or date paste)
- 3 tbsp of orange blossom water
- ½ tsp ground cinnamon
- 6 tbsp neutral oil
- 1 tbsp walnuts, finely chopped
- ½ cup (120 ml) of water with 1 tsp orange blossom water
- neutral oil (not olive oil)
- 1 cup honey (340 g) (with 1 tsp orange blossom water optional)
- toasted sesame seeds to decorate

This is another type of fried honey pastry common to Jews and Muslims from Morocco, and this recipe dates back to thirteenth-century al-Andalus. These tasty pastries flavored with honey and dates are now associated with the holidays: Muslims eat maqrūṭ *when breaking the fast of the Ramadan, and Sephardim of Morocco and France eat them for Rosh HaShana. This Jewish holiday corresponds to the Jewish New Year, and in celebration Sephardim traditionally eat sweet dishes like apples dipped in honey or dates.* Maqrūṭ *are also eaten for Hanukkah.*

In a large bowl, mix together semolina, salt, and butter until the fat is absorbed.

Meanwhile, prepare the date filling: chop the dates very finely and put them in a saucepan. Add the orange blossom water, cinnamon, and neutral oil. Cook over medium heat for about 5 minutes. Add the chopped walnuts. Mix and set aside in the fridge for 2 hours.

Then, add the ½ cup water flavored with orange blossom water to the semolina and butter, mixing with the tips of your fingers.

Divide the dough in 4 parts, and make rolls about 1 inch (2-3 cm) in diameter and 9 inches long (20 cm).

With your index finger (or a knife), make a slit length-wise in the center of each roll, without cutting through it.

Roll a little date paste and put it in the slit.

Close the edges of the dough over the date paste and seal. All the stuffing needs to be covered. Prepare all the long rolls in the same way.

Take the rolls and flatten them until they are 0.4 inches (1 cm) thick. Cut into lozenges about 1.5 inch long (2.5 cm). Take a knife and draw marks like a star.

Pour some neutral oil into a frying pan until it is 1.5 inches deep (3 cm). Heat over medium heat.

Fry the first side of the *maqrūṭ* for 2-3 minutes, and then fry the other side for another 2 minutes.

Pour the honey and blossom water into a saucepan.

Once hot (not boiling), immerse the *maqrūṭ* carefully into the warm honey for at least 3 minutes.

Be careful when you take them out as they will be soft.

Line a plate with baking parchment and put the fried *maqrūṭ* over it. Sprinkle immediately with toasted sesame seeds.

Hojuelas, fazuelos or fijuelas

Serves 10 pieces
Time: 40 minutes

- 2 cups (300 g) flour
- 1 tsp baking powder
- 3 eggs, beaten
- ½ cup (50 g) sugar
- 2 tsp water
- ½ tsp salt
- 7 tsp neutral oil
- neutral oil for frying

For the syrup:

- ½ cup (100 ml) water
- ¼ cup (50 ml) orange blossom water
- ½ cup (100 g) sugar

To decorate:

- ½ cup (50 g) icing sugar
- ¼ cup (30 g) sesame seeds

*This dish takes us on a long journey from Spain to Argentina. All Sephardim are familiar with these rolled thin strips of pastry that are quickly fried and deliciously covered in sugar: they are impossibly tender and will melt in your mouth. Though they are known under many names (*fijuelas, fazuelos, hojuelas*), their characteristic shape is always undeniably reminiscent of Esther's* meguillah, *the scroll read during the Jewish holiday of Purim, which is when* hojuelas *are traditionally prepared.*

So, in memory of Esther's story and prowess, roll up your sleeves, warm up your wrists, and get ready to prepare these wonderful hojuelas. *These will be tastier and smoother if you prepare the dough the day before frying it.*

Put the flour, the baking powder, the beaten eggs, the sugar, the water, the salt, and the oil in a bowl and mix with a spoon. Finish mixing with your hands. The dough should be smooth, without lumps.

Wrap the dough in plastic film and cool for 15 minutes.

Sprinkle flour on your working surface and roll out the dough. It must be thin and not sticky.

Cut strips 1 generous inch (3 cm) wide and about 15 inches (40 cm) long.

Heat the oil over medium heat.

Take a strip in your hand. Gently stick the teeth of a fork into one end of the strip, and put the fork in the oil to cook this portion of the strip while keeping the rest out of the pan. Small bubbles will form on the dough. Every two seconds, gently turn the fork to roll up a little more of the strip, and fry that bit. Continue like this until the entire strip of dough has been wrapped around the fork and fried.

Set aside and continue in the same way for all *hojuelas*.

Prepare the syrup: pour the water, orange blossom and sugar into a pan. Mix everything over low heat for 5 minutes. The mixture should remain very liquid and transparent.

Soak the *hojuelas* in the sugar syrup, being careful not to break them, and put them onto a serving dish.

Put the sesame seeds and the icing sugar in two separate plates, and dip one side of each *hojuela* into one or the other alternately.

I love using recipes from the Spanish late Middle Ages, adapting them while remaining as close as possible to the original method, and incorporating the typical Sephardic culinary twist. However, hojuelas *are so meaningful and full of history that we cannot change them; in fact, we* should not *change them. The term* hojuela *(from* hoja*, "very thin sheet") existed as early as 1495, in the dictionary of Nebrija, but the first written record of the term being used in a culinary context is from the sixteenth century, not from a cookbook but from the famous story* La Lozana Andaluza *we mentioned earlier by Francisco Delicado, where the protagonist Aldonza describes preparing* hojuelas *in her native Andalusia.*

Nowadays, Sephardim from Argentina and the diaspora prepare hojuelas *for Purim and also Yom Kippur. In Spain, they are eaten for Purim by Jews, but also by non-Jews during the* Semana Santa*—a Christian festival that always takes place within a few days of Purim. In fact,* hojuelas *were introduced in some Christian Spanish cookbooks as early as 1599.*

Rice and honey pudding

Serves 4
Time: 40 minutes
(plus all night)

- 5 cups (1,2 l) water
- 1 cup (210 g) short-grain rice
- ½ tsp salt
- 1 cinnamon stick
- 2 ½ (0,5 l) whole milk
- ½ cup (170 g) honey
- ⅛ cup (25 g) butter
- ⅛ cup (13 g) sugar
- 2 tsp ground cinnamon

This Iberian thirteenth-century recipe, which appears in the Kitāb al-ṭabīẖ *as "honeyed rice," would fit perfectly in a Shavuot menu today: this holiday commemorates the giving of the Ten Commandments and food laws, and traditional food for this occasion includes dairy.*

Wash the rice and leave in water all night.

The day after, wash the rice again.

Boil the water and add in rice, salt, and the cinnamon stick. Cook at medium heat for 15 minutes.

Boil the milk in another pan.

When the rice has been boiling for 15 minutes, throw out the water and, little by little, pour the boiling milk with the cinnamon stick over it.

Cook slowly at low-medium heat for at least 10 minutes until the milk has reduced; the consistency will be similar to a pudding.

Pour in a big bowl or small individual bowls. Make a hole in the middle and place the honey and soft butter in it. Sprinkle the rice pudding with sugar and cinnamon powder.

Berenjenas confitadas con canela
Candied eggplants with cinnamon

Makes 1 large jar
Time: 2 hours

- 6 very small eggplants
- 1 tsp vinegar

For the syrup:

- 2 cups (400 ml) water
- 1 3/4 cup (350 g) sugar
- 2 cinnamon sticks (2 inches long)

This is a sweet Sephardic dish that has traveled far and wide. Mainly consumed by the Sephardim of Spain and Morocco, we find these candied eggplants with cinnamon as far as the Dominican Republic. The pleasures of food know no borders.

Prick the eggplants and boil them for 7 minutes in water (just enough to cover them), with a teaspoon of vinegar. Then, put them in clean cold water for 5 minutes.

To make the syrup, gently heat water, sugar, and cinnamon in a pan. Do not let it boil.

When the syrup is hot, add the eggplants and cook them very slowly for at least 1 hour. Do not let the syrup dry out and make sure the eggplants are always submerged. Avoid touching them as they will be very soft and breakable: move the pan instead.

Submerge a jar in boiling water for 1 minute. Then, get it out and place the candied eggplants in it to keep, or eat them right away.

Neulas encanonadas
Brik pastry rolls with almonds and honey

Makes 25 pieces
Time: 1 hour

- 2 cups (230 g) ground almonds
- ½ cup (110 g) sugar
- ⅛ tsp bitter almond essence
- ¼ tsp orange blossom water
- 1 egg
- 15 brick pastry sheets (round)
- 1 cup (340 g) honey
- ¼ to ½ cup (35 g to 70 g) sesame seeds (preferably toasted)
- neutral oil (for frying)

In Le Roman d'Esther, *written in the fourteenth century by Crescas du Caylar, a Jewish physician from southern France, there is a mention of a banquet held by King Ahasuerus in honor of the third year of his reign. Crescas mentions a dish called* neulas encanonadas*: a pastry confection in the shape of cigars. Another reference to the dish comes from the Spanish city of Almazan, where* conversos *were reported to the Inquisition tribunal for preparing* rollillos *(rolls) during Semana Santa, a feast whose dates coincide with Pessah.*

In a bowl, combine the ground almonds, sugar, bitter almond essence, orange blossom water, and egg. Chill for 15 minutes.

Take the brick pastry sheets and cut them in half down the middle, using a knife. Take one half and place it so that the round side is to the left.

Heat the oil in a saucepan over medium heat.

Pour the honey in another saucepan and heat it over low heat (it must never boil).

Prepare a tray for the rolls and a small plate with sesame seeds in it.

Take the almond mix out of the refrigerator. Take the equivalent of 1 tbsp of dough and roll it into a ball. Then, shape it into a sausage (see Figure 1).

Place it a finger's width away from the edge and start rolling the pastry sheet tightly (see Figure 2).

Then, fold the two edges of the sheet inward (see Figure 3). Continue rolling to the end, keeping the edges in (see Figure 4). Do the same for all pastry sheet halves until you run out of almond mix.

Fry the rolls in the oil for about 3 minutes, turning them.

Take each out of the oil and soak it in the hot honey for 3 minutes.

Take out of the honey and coat with the sesame seeds. Cover all sides.

Place the rolls on the tray and serve.

Figure 1

Figure 2

Figure 3

Figure 4

Maimonides Cake

Serves 6
Time: 1 hour

- 12 egg whites, beaten until stiff
- ½ cup (110 g) sugar
- 1 tsp salt
- 1 lemon, juice and zest
- 1 ½ cup (250 g) flour or wheat starch
- icing sugar to sprinkle
- honey (to dip)

The Kitāb al-ṭabīḫ *contains a recipe called* Rās Maimūn, *meaning "Maimonides' head" in Arabic. This dish corresponds to a cake still made today, the* bollo Maimón *or Maimonides cake. It is nowadays a specialty of the Spanish cities of Salamanca and Zamora, and it even has its own entry in the dictionary of the Real Academia Española (2018), as "a ring of brioche dough." The shape of the baking pan is atypical for a medieval cookbook, as the edges are high and it has a cylinder in its center, like a bundt tin, so that melted honey and butter can be poured into the central hole left in the cake.*

Preheat the oven to 330°F (170°C) and butter an angel cake pan.

Whip the egg whites up at medium speed. Add the sugar gradually. Then, add the salt and lemon juice. Whip them until they start to form fairly soft peaks.

Then, add the sifted flour and the lemon zest.

Fold in delicately with a spatula.

Pour the mixture into the baking tin and bake for about 30 to 40 minutes.

As you remove it from the oven, and turn it upside down. Let it cool, uncovered.

Serve sprinkled with icing sugar, and with a small bowl of hot honey on the side, to dip the cake in. It is also delicious with milk.

Hélène Jawhara
SEPHARDI : COOKING THE

MY RECIPES BASED ON HISTORICAL SOURCES

"It is convenient to fill the stomach with pleasant and light foods to digest."

Maimonides,
Book of Asthma, Chapter VI (late twelfth century)

Manioc cheese balls with candied *pimentas biquinho vermelhas*

Makes 10
Time: 45 min

- 1 manioc (cassava) root
- 2 tsp salt
- 150 g (5,3 oz) cubed cheese like Edam
- neutral oil for frying
- 1 handful fresh cilantro leaves

For the candied *pimentas biquinho vermelhas*:

- ½ cup (100 ml) water
- ½ cup (100 g) sugar
- 10 candied pimentas biquinho vermelhas (tomato marmalade could be substituted)

After giving a talk at the University of São Paulo (USP) in Brazil, I had the idea to make this dish with traditional Brazilian ingredients.

Peel the manioc, removing the thin bark. Finely grate it and put it in a bowl. Add the salt, mix and cover. Leave in the fridge for 20 minutes.

Next, squeeze the grated manioc to remove all the water.

Heat the oil in a deep fryer or large deep pan.

Take some grated manioc, enough to make a golf ball with it; make a hole in the middle and put a cheese cube in. Close the ball and squeeze, making sure the cheese is tucked inside and no longer visible. Do the same with the rest of the mixture.

Fry the manioc cheese balls in the oil. Wait 30 seconds before moving them, then turn to cook on all sides. Transfer them to some absorbent paper.

Place the manioc cheese balls on a plate with fresh cilantro leaves and candied *pimentas biquinho vermelhas* on top (if you cannot find those you could use tomato marmalade to dip the manioc balls in). Eat hot.

To make candied *pimentas biquinho vermelhas*:

In a saucepan, gently boil ½ cup of water and ½ cup of sugar. Add the *pimentas biquinho vermelhas*. Mix gently for 15 minutes until they are translucent.

Cottage cheesecake

Serves 6
Time: 1 hour 30 minutes + overnight

- 5 eggs, separated
- ½ tsp salt
- 24 oz (750 g) cottage cheese
- 4 oz (100 g) potato cornstarch
- 1 cup (200 g) sugar
- ⅔ cup (150 ml) liquid whole cream
- Zest of ½ lemon

This is my favorite cottage cheese cheesecake for Shavuot. It is lighter than the traditional New York cheesecake, but nonetheless extremely luscious.

Preheat the oven at 375°F (190°C).

Beat all the egg whites with the salt. Put the egg yolks in another bowl.

In a separate bowl, mix together all the cottage cheese, potato cornstarch, sugar, liquid whole cream, lemon zest, and the 5 egg yolks. Slowly, add the beaten egg whites.

Pour in a greased 8-inch (20 cm) pan.

Bake in the oven at 375°F (190°C) for 35–40 minutes.

Let it cool for 1 hour, then put it in the fridge overnight before serving.

Batbot
Flat chewy Moroccan bread

Makes 6 large or 12 small flatbreads
Time: 30 minutes + 30 minutes + 30 minutes

- 4 cups (600 g) flour
- 4 cups (600 g) extra fine semolina
- 1 tbsp salt
- 2 tbsp (35 g) fresh yeast (or 1 ½ tbsp active dry yeast, or 3 tbsp sourdough starter)
- 3 ⅓ cup (670 ml) lukewarm water
- nigella seeds, sesame seeds, and za'atar to sprinkle

Flatbreads were very common in the Middle Ages in the Western and Eastern territories. This one is a very popular bread in Morocco today: commonly known as batbot, *this bread is cooked in a cast iron skillet and eaten on its own or with cheese or ground meat stuffing. I usually sprinkle it with za'atar and nigella seeds.*

In the bowl of a stand mixer, put the flour, extra fine semolina, and salt. Mix with the hook for 1 minute. Add the crumbled fresh yeast, and gradually the lukewarm water (in 4 batches).

The dough will be a bit sticky but that is normal. You should continue to mix at least for 10 minutes. If you do not have a stand mixer, knead by hand for at least 20 minutes.

Line a tray or a towel with baking paper, sprinkling with a little flour.

Take chunks of dough the size of tennis balls and knead them again until they are very smooth.

On a lightly floured surface, flatten the balls with your fingers to form round disks. Place them on the tray, sprinkled with a little flour, and cover with a kitchen towel. Leave to prove for 30 minutes.

Heat a skillet (cast iron is ideal) over medium-high heat.

Gently, take a flatbread and place it in the hot skillet.

Lightly wet your hand and gently moisten the top of the bread. Sprinkle with sesame, za'atar or nigella seeds. After 2 minutes, gently turn the bread over and cook the other side. It just needs to be golden.

These are excellent served still hot with cream cheese.

Tortitas de acelga
Chickpea flour croquettes with Swiss chard

Makes 25
Time: 40 minutes

- 1 bunch of Swiss chard
- 1 garlic clove, crushed
- ½ tsp baking powder
- 1 egg
- 1 saffron strand (or ⅛ tsp yellow food coloring)
- ½ tsp salt
- 2 ¾ cups (250 g) chickpea flour
- 1 ¼ cup (250 ml) water
- neutral oil for frying

This recipe combines some of the main ingredients of Sephardic cuisine from Spain: Swiss chard, eggs, garlic and olive oil. It is made with chickpea flour; a perfect dish for Passover.

Wash the chard and separate the green leaves only (the stalks can be used for another dish). Boil some salted water and cook them for 4 minutes. Drain and rinse them with cold water to keep them green, and squeeze them to remove all the water.

In a bowl, mix the crushed garlic, baking powder, egg, saffron and salt with a spoon.

Finely cut the chard with a knife. Add it to the bowl, followed by the chickpea flour.

Finally, pour in the water little by little. The preparation must remain a little thick.

Heat the oil over medium heat in a frying pan.

Take a spoonful of the mixture, and with two spoons form small croquettes. Fry for 2 minutes on each side. Put them on a paper towel before serving.

Pão de queijo
Tapioca cheese balls

Makes 30
Time: 30 minutes

- 2 cup (250 g) tapioca flour or tapioca starch
- 1 tsp salt
- ⅓ cup + 1 tbsp (100 ml) milk
- 3 tbsp (35 ml) neutral oil
- 1 cup (100 g) grated parmesan cheese
- 1 ½ cup (100 g) grated cheese such as Emmental
- 2 eggs
- Poppy seeds, flax seeds, sesame seeds (optional)

In English, "pão de queijo" is translated into "cheese bread." This chewy ball made without wheat flour or yeast has cheese as its main ingredient, and it is one of Brazil's most iconic dishes. An interesting point is that the shape and taste of this dish resembles the muğabbana *that we have already mentioned in this book. Its ingredients are perfect for Passover.*

Adaptation is a word that characterizes Jewish food. The fact that the Sephardim who fled Spain to Brazil decided to prepare their cheese ball with tapioca flour—the Brazilian vegetable par excellence*—is the most probable hypothesis for the creation of this dish.*

Preheat the oven at 375°F (190°C).

Put the tapioca flour or starch and the salt in a big bowl.

Pour the milk and oil into a saucepan. Once it starts boiling, take it off the heat and pour over the flour/salt preparation. Mix all with a spoon and then add the two grated cheeses.

Finally, add the two eggs and mix all together using a spoon. Then mix by hand. You can add seeds if you want the *pão de queijo* to be a little crunchy. Make balls the size of walnuts.

Lay the *pão de queijo* on a baking tray lined with parchment paper. Bake for 12–13 minutes and serve hot.

Rose apple tart

Serves 6
Time: 1 hour

For the dough:

- 1 ⅓ cup (180 g) flour
- ½ cup (110 g) butter, soft
- 1 ½ cup (140 g) icing sugar
- 2 egg yolks
- 2 ½ tbsp cornstarch
- 1 tsp honey
- 8 chopped dates

For the apples:

- 5 apples, ideally a mix of Braeburn and Granny Smith (avoid Golden Delicious)
- 1 cup (200 ml) water
- 1 tbsp lemon juice
- ¼ cup (25 g) ground almonds
- 1 tbsp sugar

To sprinkle:

- 2 tsp sugar
- 2 tsp honey

This dish is perfect as an original dessert for Rosh HaShana. It represents a flower that opens to welcome the New Year, with apples and dates bathed in honey so that, as per tradition, the year is sweet.

Start with the dough: in a big bowl, mix flour, soft butter, icing sugar, egg yolks, starch and honey with a wooden spoon. Add the very finely chopped dates.

With your fingertips, finish mixing and form a ball. Wrap it in plastic and put it in the fridge for 30 minutes.

Meanwhile, prepare the apples: wash them but do not peel them. Slice them into large slivers (like large rose petals), vertically. Place them in a bowl with 1 cup of water and the lemon juice.

Cover the bowl with plastic wrap and cook in the microwave for 5 minutes.

Preheat the oven to 350°F (180°C), and prepare a tart ring 8 or 9 inches (20 or 22 cm) in diameter: butter it and sprinkle with icing sugar.

Roll out the dough between two sheets of baking paper until it is a little wider than the diameter of the tart tin.

Peel off the baking sheet from the top of the dough and transfer it to the tin, pressing it down lightly. Do not remove the dough that protrudes (you will do that once the tart is baked).

Take the apples: pat dry each slice on a paper towel, before starting to layer them inside the edge of the tart tin. Make each slice overlap a little on the previous, like the petals of a rose.

Do the same with all the slices, sprinkling a little ground almonds and sugar between them as you go.

Bake for 30 minutes. Once out of the oven, sprinkle with sugar and honey. Only remove it from the tin when completely cold.

Spinach *mina*

Serves 6
Time: 45 minutes

- 1 ¼ pound (600 g) fresh spinach
- 1 ½ cup (150 g) grated cheese
- 3 eggs
- 1 white onion, cut into strips
- 1 cup (225 g) heavy cream
- 2 tsp salt
- 2 tsp black pepper
- 2 puff pastry sheets (1 pound in total), very thinly rolled out
- egg wash
- za'atar and sesame seeds to sprinkle

This recipe is very popular among the Sephardic communities around the world, especially those from Greece, Turkey, and the South Balkans. The mina *is delicious when made with Swiss chard as well.*

Cook the spinach in boiling water for 15 minutes and drain it.

In a bowl, mix the cheese, eggs, onion, cream, salt, and pepper. Add the spinach.

Place one puff pastry sheet in a baking tin, spreading it up the sides. Prick the dough with a fork. Add the spinach mixture.

Cover with the other puff pastry sheet, pinching the edges to seal the dough.

Brush with egg wash and sprinkle with za'atar and sesame seeds.

Bake at 350°F (180°C) for 40 minutes, until the top is golden brown.

Let it rest for 30 minutes before serving.

ACKNOWLEDGEMENTS

The publication of this book has been possible with the support of the American Sephardi Federation and its executive director Jason Guberman-Pfeffer. I would also like to thank the scientific council of the IEHCA (European Institute of History and Culture of Food) for their financial support towards publication. I am especially grateful to Alessandra Anzani, the Editorial Director at Academic Studies Press for her patience, support and enthusiasm in this project, to Production Editor Kira Nemirovsky, and to Matthew Charlton and Jenna Colozza, ASP's Marketing and Sales team. I would also like to thank the documentary consultation service of the General Archives of the Nation (AGN) of Mexico for their help in accessing the various manuscripts.

A special mention goes to David Gitlitz, whose fame as a historian and specialist in crypto-Jews is unparalleled. He passed away three weeks after writing the foreword to this book. I met him at the Society for Crypto-Judaic Studies in Philadelphia in 2017. His wisdom, his kindness and his willingness to share his knowledge made me admire him. I am proud to be his friend. Warm thanks to my friend Candice Kiss who, since our meeting at the conference organized by the SCJS, has always been present, advising me and supporting me in my career, and in the preparation of this cookbook. The same goes for my friend Estrella Abudarham, with whom I have regularly shared my ideas, and for all the people who—without having met them in person—have virtually shared a slice of Sephardic culinary life. I also warmly thank my husband and my children for their patience and for having at times tested ten different dishes on the same day. Finally, I have deep gratitude, recognition, pride, and love for my grandmother, Ana Guillen Palma, who always believed in me and transmitted her passion for cooking to me.

BIBLIOGRAPHY

Abbott, Lyman, and Thomas Jefferson Conant. *A Dictionary of Religious Knowledge, for Popular and Professional Use: Comprising Full Information on Biblical, Theological, and Ecclesiastical Subjects. With Several Hundred Maps and Illustrations*. New York: Harper & Brothers, 1885.

Abreu (de), Capistrano. *Primeira Visitacao Do Santo Officio as Partes Do Brasil Pelo Licenciado Heiter Furtads de Mendoca: Confissoes Da Bahia, 1591–92*. Lenox, MA: Hardpress Publishing, 2013.

Baena (de), Juan Alfonso. *El Cancionero. (Siglo XV): Ahora por primera vez dado a luz, con notas y comentarios*. Madrid: La Publicidad, 1851.

Baer, Yitzhak. *Historia de los judios en la España cristiana*. Barcelona: Riopiedras, 1998.

Beinart, Haim. *Records of Trials of the Spanish Inquisition in Ciudad Real, vol. 1: 1483–1485*. Jerusalem: Israel National Academy of Sciences and Humanities, 1974.

———. *Records of Trials of the Spanish Inquisition in Ciudad Real, vol. 2: 1494–1512*. Jerusalem: Israel National Academy of Sciences and Humanities, 1977.

———. *Records of Trials of the Spanish Inquisition in Ciudad Real, vol. 3: 1512–1527*. Jerusalem: Israel National Academy of Sciences and Humanities, 1981.

Bos, Gerrit, ed. *Maimonides on the Regimen of Health: A New Parallel*. Leiden: Brill, 2019.

Bravo Lledó, Pilar. "Las costumbres judeoconversas en Alcalá de Henares." Museo Casa Natal de Cervantes, Archivo Histórico Nacional, 2012.

Buresi, Pascal. "L'Empire Almohade. Le Maghreb et Al-Andalus (1130–1269)." In *Les Empires. Antiquités et Moyen Âge. Analyse comparée*, edited by F. Hurlet, 221–237. Rennes: Presses Universitaires de Rennes, 2008.

Carrete Parondo, Carlos, and Carolina Fraile Conde. *Fontes Iudaeorum Regni Castellae, vol. 4: Los judeoconversos de Almazán (1501–1505). Origen familiar de los Lainez*. Salamanca: Universidad Pontificada de Salamanca and Universidad de Granada, 1987.

Carrete Parondo, Carlos. *Fontes Iudaeorum Regni Castellae, vol. 2: El Tribunal de la Inquisición en el Obispado de Soria (1486–1502)*. Salamanca: Universidad Pontificada de Salamanca and Universidad de Granada, 1985.

———. *Fontes Iudaeorum Regni Castellae, vol. 3: Proceso inquisitorial contra los Arias Dávila segovianos: un enfrentamiento social entre judíos y conversos*. Salamanca: Universidad Pontificada de Salamanca and Universidad de Granada, 1986.

Cooper, John. *Eat and be Satisfied: A Social History of Jewish Food*. Lanham, MD Jason Aronson, 1993.

Diccionario Histórico (1933–1936). https://webfrl.rae.es/DH1936.html

Eguilaz y Yanguas (de), Leopoldo. *Glosario etimológico de las palabras españolas de origen oriental*. Granada: Edition La Lealtad, 1886.

Escobar Quevedo, Ricardo. *Inquisición y Judaizantes en América Española (Siglos XVI–XVII)*. Bogotá: Universidad del Rosario, 2010.

Gitlitz, David, and Linda Kay Davidson. *A Drizzle of Honey.* New York: Saint Martin's Press, 1999.

Gitlitz, David. *Secrecy and Deceit. The Religion of the Crypto-Jews*. Philadelphia: The Jewish Publication Society, 1996.

Guillaumond, Catherine. *Cuisine et diététique dans l'Occident arabe médiéval. D'après un traité anonyme du XIIIe siècle. Étude et traduction française.* Paris: L'Harmattan, 2017.

Hajjar, Rachel. "The Air of History. Part III: The Golden Age in Arab Islamic Medicine. An Introduction." *Heart Views: The Official Journal of the Gulf Heart Association 14, no. 1 (January–March 2013): 43–46.*

Huici Miranda, Ambrosio. *La cocina hispano-magrebí en la época almohade Según un manuscrito anónimo del siglo XIII*. Introduction by Manuela Marín. Gijón: Trea, 2005.

Humash, Edmond J. Safra Edition: The Torah, Haftarot, and Five Megillot with a Commentary from Rabbinic Writings. New York: ArtScroll Mesorah Publications, 2017.

Ibn Razīn al-Tuǧībī. *Relieves de las mesas acerca de las delicias de la comida y los diferentes platos (Fuḍālat al-Ḫiwān fī ṭayyibāt al-ṭa'ām wa-l-alwān).* Edited, translated, and with notes by Manuela Marín. Gijón: Trea, 2007.

Jawhara Piñer, Hélène. "Maqruḍ المقروض or Maqrūṭ المقروط: A Moroccan Sephardi Recipe for Ramadan." The *Sephardi World Weekly*, No. 182, 1 June 2018. Available from: http://eepurl.com/dwVZBf

———. "Making Mufleta, History's Oldest Jewish Pastry, for the Holidays." *Tablet Magazine*, September 7, 2018.

———. "Almoronía: A Moroccan-Jewish Recipe from the 13th Century Andalusia." *The Sephardi Report*, Vol. 6, no. 1 (Spring 2019): 78.

———. "Between Health and Pleasure, the Culinary Recipes of the *Kitāb al-ṭabīḫ*." *Conceφtos* (University of Bordeaux-Montaigne (France)), forthcoming Spring 2022.

———. "El patrimonio culinario judío de la Península Ibérica a través de un manuscrito del siglo XIII. Ejemplos de la pervivencia de recetas en la cocina de los sefardíes de España y de Marruecos." *Ladinar,* XII: 45–62.

———. "A Jewish Dish of Chicken, an Andalusian recipe لون من فروج يهودى." *University of Toronto Journal of Jewish Thought*, forthcoming Fall 2022.

———. *Jews, Food and Spain: Evolution and Transmission of the Spanish Jewish Culinary Heritage from the 12th Century to the Sephardic Diaspora*. Boston: Academic Studies Press, Spring 2022.

———. "Le patrimoine culinaire de l'Espagne actuelle au travers des livres de cuisine anciens : évolution et permanence de la pratique de certaines recettes." In *Actes du 143e Congrès national des sociétés historiques et scientifiques "La transmission des savoirs, Transmettre un savoir-faire": 23–27 avril 2018*. Paris: Éditions du CTHS, forthcoming 2022.

Maimonides. *Hanhagat ha-Beri'ut (Regimen Sanitatis).* Edited by Solomon Munter. Jerusalem: Mosad ha-Rav Kook, 1957.

———. *Moses Maimonides' Two Treatises on the Regimen of Health: Fī Tadbīr al-Sihhah and Maqālah fi Bayān Ba'd al-A'rād wa-al-Jawāb 'anhā*. Edited and translated by Ariel Bar-Sela, Hebbel E. Hoff, Elias Faris. *Transactions of the American Philosophical Society* 54, no. 4 (1964): 3–50.

———. *Obras médicas, vol. 1: El régimen de salud. Tratado sobre la curación de las hemorroides*. Edited and translated by Lola Ferre. Barcelona: Herder, 2016.

———. *Obras médicas, vol. 2: El libro del asma*. Edited and translated by Lola Ferre. Barcelona: Herder, 2016.

Michel, Francisque, ed. *El Cancionero de Juan Alfonso de Baena, vol. 2.* Leipzig: Brockhaus, 1860.

Nirenberg, David. *Neighboring Faiths: Christianity, Islam, and Judaism in the Middle Ages and Today*. Chicago: University of Chicago Press, 2014.

Pérez Alonso, María Isabel. "La olla judía del Šabbat: Estudio lexicológico y lexicográfico de adafina, Ḥamín, caliente(s) y otras denominaciones." *Espacio, tiempo y forma, series 3: Historia Medieval 28* (2015): 441–458.

Perry, Charles. "The Description of Familiar Foods." In *Medieval Arab Cookery*, edited by A. J. Arberry, Maxime Rodinson, and Charles Perry, foreword by Claudia Roden, 273–465. Totnes: Prospect Books, 2006.

Picard, Christophe. "L'âge d'or de l'Islam." *L'Histoire* 260 (December 2001): 46–47.

Qusṭā ibn Lūqā's medical regime for the pilgrims to Mecca: Risālā fī tadbīr safar al-ḥajj. Translated and edited by Gerrit Bos. New York: Brill, 1992.

Rodinson, Maxime, A. J. Arberry, and Charles Perry. *Medieval Arab Cookery*. Totnes: Prospect Books, 2006.

Romero Castelló, Elena. "El olor del sábado: La adafina, del Arcipreste de Hita a las versiones 'light.'" In *La mesa puesta: leyes, costumbres y recetas judías: XVI curso de cultura hispanojudía y sefardí de la Universidad de Castilla-La Mancha: En memoria de Iacob M. Hassán*, edited by Uriel Macías and Ricardo Izquierdo Benito. Cuenca: Universidad de Castilla la Mancha, 2010: 215–240.

Sánchez Moya, Manuel, and Jasone Monasterio Aspiri. "Los judaizantes turolenses en el siglo XV." *Sefarad* 32, 2 (1972): 307–340.

Santanach, Joan, Mònica Barrieras, Antoni Riera, and Ramón Banegas. *Libre de Sent Soví*. Barcelona: Barcino, 2014.

Shatzmiller, Maya. "Professions and Ethnic Origin of Urban Labourers in Muslim Spain: Evidence from a Moroccan Source." *Awraq* 5 (1983): 152–153.

Siqueira, Sonia. *A Inquisição portuguesa e a sociedade colonial: a açao do Santo Oficio na Bahia e em Pernambuco na época das visitações*. São Paulo: Atica, 1978.

Toaff, Ariel. "Le couscous et l'histoire des juifs en Italie." In *Couscous, boulgour et polenta. Transformer et consommer les céréales dans le monde, edited by* Hélène Franconie, Monique Chastanet et François Sigaut, 143–144. Paris: Karthala, 2010.

Toro, Alfonso, ed. *Los judíos en la Nueva España: documentos del siglo XVI correspondientes al ramo de Inquisición.* Mexico City: Archivo General de la Nación, Fondo de cultura económica, 1982.

Uchmany, Eva Alexandra. *La vida entre el judaísmo y el cristianismo en la Nueva España (1580–1606).* Mexico City: Archivo General de la Nación, 1992.

Valérian, Dominique. *Islamisation et arabisation de l'Occident musulman médiéval (VIIe–XIIe siècle).* Paris: Publications de la Sorbonne, 2011.

Wachtel, Nathan. *Entre Moïse et Jésus. Études marranes (XVe–XXIe siècle)*. Paris: CNRS Éditions, 2013.

Yerushalmi, Yosef Hayim. *Sefardica.* Paris: Chandeigne, 1998 (2nd ed. 2016).

LIST OF ILLUSTRATIONS

All photographs by the author

INDEX

About the Author

Hélène Jawhara Piñer holds a doctoral degree in Medieval History and the History of Food from the University of Tours, France. She was awarded the Broome & Allen Fellowship from the American Sephardi Federation in 2018 and the David Gitlitz Emerging Scholar Prize from the Society for Crypto-Judaic Studies in 2021, both dedicated to recognizing academic accomplishments and service on behalf of the Sephardic community and for encouraging continued excellence in the field of Sephardi Studies and Crypto-Judaic Studies.

She is a research associate at the Centre for Advanced Studies in the Renaissance (CESR) of Tours, France. Her main research interests include the medieval culinary history of Spain through inter- and multiculturalism, with a special focus on Jewish culinary heritage. Her articles have been published in multiple international journals such as *Meldar*, *Ladinar*, *eHumanista*, and *Conceptos*, as well as mainstream media such as *Sephardi World Weekly*, *Tablet Magazine*, and *The Forward*. The *Los Angeles Times* published an in-depth article on the importance of *Sephardi: Cooking the Jewish History* for Sephardi culture. In May 2020, Dr. Jawhara Piñer attended "The Great Big Jewish Food Fest" as a presenter for a historical-cooking demonstration. From 2020-2021, she spearheaded the live culinary show "Sephardic Culinary History with chef Hélène Jawhara Piñer", which included thirteen sessions promoted by the American Sephardi Federation and The Center of Jewish History.

Dr. Jawhara-Piñer is also the author of the academic monograph *Jews, Food, and Spain: Evolution and Transmission of the Spanish Jewish Culinary Heritage from the 12th Century to the Sephardic Diaspora*, forthcoming in spring 2022.

Also by Hélène Jawhara Piñer

Jews, Food, and Spain
Evolution and Transmission of the Spanish Jewish Culinary Heritage
from the 12th Century to the Sephardic Diaspora

(Academic Studies Press, 2022)

helenejawharapiner

www.helenejawharapiner.com

“This book comes with a heart, a spine, a soul. Its spine is the resilience of a thousand years of Sephardi cooks, living in minority enclaves surrounded by frequently unfriendly majority cultures, who retained the essence of their Jewish culinary heritage and transmitted it to their children. Its heart beats to the rhythms of the Jewish week and liturgical year, Shabbat, Sukkot, Pesach, Yom Kippur, the fasts and feasts, the tables around which Jewish families gathered from season to season and from century to century. Its soul is nurtured in a faith that despite the hatred and fear, the Inquisitions and the pogroms, the silent discriminations and the attractions of assimilation, Sephardi descendants in Spain, in Portugal, and in all the lands of the diaspora are, and will forever be, cooking Jewish.”

— David M. Gitlitz, Professor Emeritus of Hispanic studies, and co-author of *A Drizzle of Honey*

“The gorgeously illustrated book, accompanied by uncomplicated instructions, offers dishes with spices and herbs, some similar to those in Middle Eastern cooking. Several of the author’s personal recipes are drawn from historical sources adapted from her academic research.”

— Jane Manaster, *San Francisco Book Review*

“Sephardic Jewish culture was important not only in the Iberian peninsula, but in a vast international diaspora, especially in the modern age. Historical investigation of primary sources uses texts, images, artifacts and other documents to analyze the past. The history of food has a fundamental repertoire for getting to know the food of yore: cookbooks. The work of the historian Hélène Jawhara Piñer retrieves the most important medieval and modern recipes of Sephardic food to reconstruct these dishes and understand them as part of a persecuted culture that maintained its identity based on the precepts of kashrut, the Jewish commandments, but, in the face of anti-Semitism and of the Inquisition, he also often had to hide his Jewish condition in order to survive.

A kitchen that reveals and hides, expresses and delimits identities, serves as a border landmark of belonging to a community. In this universe, Jawhara Piñer not only observes, but tastes, when rereading the recipes not only with a look, but through the contemporary experimentation of the old recipes.

The result is an extraordinary book, which unravels the Sephardic past with the lenses of a cook historian, who not only reads the story, but cooks it over a slow fire, like the one needed for Shabbat dishes remained warm.”

— Henrique Soares Carneiro, Professor of Modern History, University of São Paulo

“Reading these recipes I could almost smell my grandmother’s kitchen, and the dishes she cooked which descended from the Sephardic community in Smyrna. Jawhara Piñer’s research has uncovered details that have been mostly forgotten, and I am certain that this book will have readers running to the stove to taste this largely unknown, opulent cuisine.”

— Ken Albala, Professor of History, University of the Pacific

“A vibrant scholar and a very talented cook, Hélène Jawhara Piñer has written a brilliant book that is as appealing as it is enlightening. From showing us that Swiss chard was mentioned in the Talmud to revealing that Jewish dishes were featured in prominent Muslim cookbooks, she makes every page one worth reading—and every recipe one you’ll want to make. Her research expands our idea of edible Sephardic culture, charting its geography and anthropology to places as far-flung as Brazil and Mexico, in the process serving up important context for an impressively rich culinary heritage. *Sephardi* reminds us that there’s always lots to learn about even the most time-honored traditions, and it’s a work that encourages us all to dig deeper into our own individual histories, no matter where in the world they originate.”

— Adeena Sussman, author of *Sababa: Fresh Sunny Flavors From My Israeli Kitchen*

“Hélène Jawhara Piñer’s *Sephardi: Cooking the History* is a critical new work of Jewish culinary history. The book sheds a much-needed light on the foods of Jews from the Iberian peninsula while elucidating the community’s rich culinary legacy. The role that ingredients, dishes, and cooking practices played in signaling one’s religious identity under the inquisition speaks to the centrality that food played—and continues to play—in Jewish life. Jawhara Piñer’s cookbook is deeply researched, and in addition to providing thorough historical context to foods commonly associated with the Sephardic diaspora, the book also provides many unique and rare recipes that bring Sephardic Jewish history to life in the kitchen.”

— Jeffrey Yoskowitz, author of *The Gefilte Manifesto*